The Teenager Is Not a Coordinated Plot
(Against a Parent's Sanity)

THE Teenager IS NOT A Coordinated Plot

(Against a Parent's Sanity)

TONYA REILLY

HOUNDSTOOTH
PRESS

COPYRIGHT © 2025 TONYA REILLY
All rights reserved.

THE TEENAGER IS NOT A COORDINATED PLOT
(AGAINST A PARENT'S SANITY)

FIRST EDITION

ISBN   978-1-5445-4804-3   *Hardcover*
       978-1-5445-4802-9   *Paperback*
       978-1-5445-4803-6   *Ebook*

To Aaron and Elizabeth,
I know I learned on your dime.

Contents

Introduction 11

Part One: The Physiology

CHAPTER 1: TEENAGE BRAIN
At a Cafeteria Table Near You..19

CHAPTER 2: SLEEP
I'll Get You a Mockingbird If You Go to Sleep 27

CHAPTER 3: APPEARANCES
Large Child? No. More Beautiful Adult?
Not that either.. 37

Part Two: The Emotions

CHAPTER 4: STABILITY
Terra Firma 51

CHAPTER 5: IMPORTANCE
They Want to Matter..61

CHAPTER 6: CONNECTION
They Need Their People 71

CHAPTER 7: DON'TS
Just Because You Have a Teenager in the House,
You Don't Have to Be an Asshole About It 77

Part Three: The Minefields

CHAPTER 8: SCHOOL
But Will It Be on the Test?..93

CHAPTER 9: PEERS
Shakespearean Dramas and Greek Tragedies 105

CHAPTER 10: SEX
Amorous Walked into a Party..................................... 113

CHAPTER 11: DRUGS
Pass the Puffer Fish 121

Conclusion... 131
And by Actual Experts.. 133
Acknowledgments 135
About the Author..137

"The world is passing through troublous times. The young people of today think of nothing but themselves. They have no reverence for parents or old age. They are impatient of all restraint. They talk as if they knew everything, and what passes for wisdom with us is foolishness with them. As for the girls, they are forward, immodest and unladylike in speech, behavior and dress."

—FROM A SERMON PREACHED BY
PETER THE HERMIT IN AD 1274

Introduction

A disagreeable teenager won't keep you up at night. It's when they are out and about God knows where with God knows who and up to God knows what that you may lie there wide awake, feeling that anger/fear mix you may have gotten altogether too familiar with.

You no longer worry about parking lots and swimming pools. But...teenage humans tend to do risky and dangerous stuff. These are the humans who keep the statistics up for nonnatural causes of death—all the headliners: accidents, drug overdoses, weapons, suicide, and murder.

All right, that's terrifying. But we're not done yet. Alcohol makes all people do stupid shit, and teenagers are already more prone to groupthink and consequence obliviousness. They are easily distracted, inexperienced drivers. And driving fast is fun. Racing is even more fun. Then there's the sex, the sexual assaults, and the sexual assaults that get filmed.

Maybe your kid has been an easy kid and seems to have a good head on their shoulders. You also know they are no more than one degree of separation from some stupid, dangerous undertakings.

One day you notice a new friend who seems a little off, a little sketchy, but you're not sure why. Maybe the grades have suddenly gone to hell. Maybe you keep catching sight of a profound sadness on your kid's face. You hold your observations up against the first couple of paragraphs herein, and you, first, are really afraid for your kid and not sure whether you are afraid enough, and next, have no idea what to do.

A control grab ain't it

As the parent of a teenage human, you have been dealt a terrifying hand. Some parents will play the hand by grasping for control. More rules, more restrictions, and more threats of punishment. The nice people at Amazon have several parenting books with "Control" in the title. Unless it is immediately followed by "Yourself," as in "Control Yourself," I don't find it a useful word. I advocate investing for influence rather than grabbing at control.

I've heard, "If you don't control them when they are little, you won't be able to control them when they are teenagers"—to which I respond, you won't be able to *control them*. Hard stop. You are out of the control game. You will not be there when they decide to drink or experiment with drugs. You will not be there when they decide whether or not to have sex, put on a condom, or insist upon a condom. You will not be there when they are asked to send a naked photo of themselves. You will not be there when they decide whether or not to get behind the wheel after drinking or into the car with a driver who has been drinking.

There are no safety guarantees, and you don't have control

over much really ever. So what the hell do you do? Although there isn't any "How to Control Your Kid" information here, there are ways to protect, build, and use your relationship to get your darling through these years as safely as possible. You can't control their choices, but you have a great deal of influence. Do not abdicate it. Be deliberate in your relationship with your teenager.

You abdicate your influence if you stockpile control strategies that ultimately undermine your relationship. You also abdicate your influence when you become paralyzed with fear, just hoping for the best.

I didn't get the degree, but I got the experience

I have two kids, now grown and launched, a boy and a girl. A friend asked, "Is the book about the stuff you did as a parent or the stuff you wished you'd done?" Both.

Neither myself nor my kids' father were model teenagers in the early eighties—we each chose drinking, drugs, smoking, and other stupidness. While this history let me know how scared I should be, it also kept me from thinking that a teenager doing teenager stuff was a bad kid destined to be a loser for life.

This perspective relieved me from attempting lockdown punishment gestapo parenting. However, I failed to double down on some suggestions in this book and provide the home base and emotional security I wish I had. My twenty-twenty hindsight informs significant portions of this book.

My father was "anti," as in anti government, anti police, anti city taxes, anti being told what to do. He once stated, without irony, "We used to drink and drive responsibly. Now the *GOVERNMENT* needs to tell us what to do." He would disparagingly say, "*EVERYONE wants to be an AUTHOR-ITY.*" With fondness for my dad, my kids and I use this line whenever we disagree with someone.

I am not an authority. It is in my genetics to question authority. I'm the irreverent, sometimes foul-mouthed friend who meets you for coffee. Much of what I have to say goes against common teen parenting advice, which is why I wrote a book. This isn't about how to deal with a problem kid. This is about building a home for, and relationship with, your kid. This is how you increase the odds against their making dangerous choices.

I would have liked this book

Any parenting books I crossed paths with when my kids were teenagers were about control, and determining if your kid needs rehab, and how to implement consequences, and how to beat your chest or whatever a strong parent was supposed to do. None of that ever rang true for me. I remember being sixteen, and parental attempts at control and consequences did not improve my decisions.

If something herein is helpful, I am so grateful. If something sounds crackers, just leave it.

I have an agenda: For you to be deliberate in the care and feeding of your teenager. For you to be deliberate in the relationship. Because I want you and your darling to have a decent base from which to deal with fraught minefield-laden topics.

You will have to invest more energy and time into raising this teenager than you might have expected. Your darling may appear as if they don't want all that much to do with you. Sometimes you may feel unwanted and unappreciated—

which is totally fine, because none of this is about you. And like everything else wonderful and awful, it does not last forever. You are responsible for raising, guiding, supporting, and loving them. They aren't responsible for making you feel loved or appreciated. They may, but they may not. It's totally fine either way.

Here's the plan: First, we'll look at your darling's brain; its best friend, sleep; and how their brain is neither the brain of a large child nor that of a more beautiful adult. Then we'll consider the components of emotional well-being—what you can do and what you very much should not do. Then we'll be as ready as we're going to get for the minefields of School, Peers, Sex, and Drugs.

Let's do this.

PART ONE

The Physiology

Long ago and far away, I read the following somewhere: It is the teenager's job to be the most self-centered, selfish creature on earth. A teenager has a developing brain and a changing body. Along with that comes a social world that used to be simple but now includes romance and sexual interest and attention. And their friends are all going through the same stuff, and everyone seems to be operating with only half an instruction book. All of this is a full-time job for them, so please don't take it personally if they don't actually give a shit about your day. It will hurt less when you see that it isn't personal—it's age-appropriate self-absorption.

Once I shared with a psychologist coworker that I just wanted my daughter to listen to me and understand why I had been so stupidly upset over something. The woman knew nothing about my daughter other than her age, sixteen. Without missing a beat, the woman responded, "Yeah. She's not going to do that." I had already resigned myself to not getting what I wanted, but her comment made this letdown not personal. Impersonal disappointments are just easier.

CHAPTER 1: TEENAGE BRAIN

At a Cafeteria Table Near You

You may ask yourself, *What the hell is going on with this kid? Why can't the kid be agreeable or rational? Why aren't they listening? Why do they sometimes seem like an idiot? Why are their friends such dipshits? And what is with the goddamn attitude all the time?*

This chapter, oversimplified for sure, looks at what's going on in the teenage brain for some answers to these questions.

Imagine a cast of characters sits down at a cafeteria table...

First, meet the teenage prefrontal cortex, herein referred to as the character PreFrontalCortex. PreFrontalCortex oversees decision-making, reasoning, and impulse control. This character is easy for a parent to like. Unfortunately, this one is weak (the teenage prefrontal cortex is not yet fully developed). This one is also socially disconnected from the rest of the characters (the teenage prefrontal cortex is not yet fully wired with the rest of the brain).

Next, meet the teenage dopamine system, the character we'll refer to as Dopamine, which heightens reward anticipation and provides the mojo to go after those rewards. This system is extra strong in the teenage brain. Teenagers have Dopamine like Luke Skywalker has the Force. The result is an elevated attraction toward excitement and novelty. This character Dopamine travels with an entourage: EasilyBored, ThrillSeeker, and Impulsive.

HighEmotions is at the table too. Emotions live in the limbic system of the brain. During adolescence the limbic area gets hit with an influx of sex hormones, which show up to grow a girl into a woman and boy into a man. You know the hormones. The ones that make premenstrual, menopausal, and pregnant women occasionally seem unhinged. Or make men aggressive and ready to throw down. (Yes, totally oversimplified and generalized, but I want to make the point quickly.) When the limbic system gets hit with high doses of estrogen, progesterone, and testosterone while the underdeveloped PreFrontalCortex isn't the calming influence it one day may be, emotions can run amok. Teenagers often gravitate toward activities with emotional intensity. When *Titanic* was the tearjerker of the day, teenagers had *Titanic*-and-Cry get-togethers. Aggression? How about an MMA fight?

Don't miss Amorous. While the sex hormones are driving HighEmotions, these hormones are also in play such that even if a teenager doesn't really want to have sex, someone else probably really wants to have sex with them. These people become preoccupied with being attractive and getting attention from potential romantic and sexual partners. Some will

> "The only thing more dangerous than a bored teenager is two bored teenagers."
>
> —KNOCK KNOCK (2015)

fantasize about being in rom-com love stories, and some will fantasize about sex.

Just meeting this crew, you can see the potential for trouble.

PreFrontalCortex is no match for this crew

You've been teaching consequences for several years by the time you have a teenager in the house. Teenagers know that people OD, get arrested, get killed in car accidents, and get pregnant. However, the mismatch of high-octane Dopamine with underdeveloped PreFrontalCortex means a consequence does not get the same decision-making weight as a prospective reward (otherwise known as a really good time). Hence, we see more impulsivity, risk tolerance, and thrill-seeking from teenagers than from other age groups.

As their total brain functioning is only about 80 percent that of an adult and they haven't had as much life experience, they aren't as quick to arrive at obvious answers. The article "Adolescents and Risk: Helping Young People Make Better Choices" by Eric Wargo examines adolescent risk evaluation: "In a recent study, people of different ages were asked to respond quickly to easy, risk-related questions like 'Is it a good idea to set your hair on fire?'...Adolescents took about a sixth of a second longer than adults to get to the obvious 'no.' A sixth of a second may not seem like a lot, but it reflects a major difference between the brains of adolescents and adults."[1]

---

[1] Eric Wargo, "Adolescents and Risk: Helping Young People Make Better Choices," ACT for Youth Center of Excellence, Cornell University, September 2007, https://actforyouth.net/resources/rf/rf_risk_0907.pdf.

The power struggle is real

Dopamine and PreFrontalCortex compete for decision-making authority. "I Want" competes against "Let's Think." This competition is in play during our adult dilemmas.

First at play, Dopamine. This character's most frequent refrain: "I Want." Dopamine LOVES a reward. Dopamine loves slot machines. People sit at slot machines, pressing play, for hours. They feed money into the noisy beasts because Dopamine says anticipating a win is fun. Actual winning just enhances Dopamine's anticipation of more winning, so there the people stay. There are people who will pee their pants rather than leave a slot machine they think is about to hit. That's never on the casino billboards. Thank God. America doesn't want to see that.

Our challenger, PreFrontalCortex. This character's most frequent refrain: "Let's Think." PreFrontalCortex likes to set budgets, evaluate consequences, and take care of themself. Here's a conversation that has played out between PreFrontalCortex and Dopamine in my own brain, and I doubt I am the only one:

Dopamine: "I want PIE."

PreFrontalCortex: "Let's Think. You aren't hungry. Your fat pants are tight."

Dopamine: "I don't care. I want PIE. NOW would be the right time."

Adults have these internal debates about all sorts of things. Pie. New Shoes. Another Drink. Another Episode. Another Hand of Blackjack. Another Slot Machine Play. And so on. Sometimes PreFrontalCortex wins and a responsible choice is made. Often Dopamine wins. How do you know? There are overweight people, credit card debt, high alcohol sales, plenty of streaming TV channels, and profitable casinos.

Dopamine often beats *ADULT* PreFrontalCortex, and adult PreFrontalCortex is fully developed and wired to the rest of the adult brain.

Back at the cafeteria table, quiet teenage PreFrontalCortex doesn't have a lot of play against teenage hopped-up triple espresso Dopamine. Dopamine strongly states, "I Want," and PreFrontalCortex quietly responds, "Let's Think." Dopamine also runs with a backup crew: EasilyBored, ThrillSeeker, and Impulsive. HighEmotions and Amorous also roll with Dopamine.

This gang of beautiful, creative, and energetic characters is happy to hang out at the table all day and into the night, stirring up drama, fun, and danger. They often give two shits what PreFrontalCortex has to say about anything. PreFrontalCortex is a late bloomer and has a hard time being loud enough to be part of the conversation. PreFrontalCortex is regularly talked over and often ignored. Poor kid.

There are many tables in the cafeteria

This cast of characters sits down at a cafeteria table among a bunch of other cafeteria tables filled with like casts of characters. And they are all really important to one another, except, of course, those poor PreFrontalCortex characters; they tend to get ignored.

Teenage peer relationships become paramount. Those peers ALSO are drawn to novelty and excitement, and ALSO don't have fully developed reasoning and judgment. They are all running around together with elevated dopamine systems, underdeveloped prefrontal cortexes, and some very strong emotions. And a lot of them want to have sex with each other.

Evolution has rewarded humans whose teen individuals

leave the cave and find their way in the world away from family. Cave-Leavers found new territories and new resources and avoided genetic inbreeding. The Cave-Leavers needed to be strong, and they needed to like excitement and risk. Leaving was risky. The Cave-Leavers needed to place more value on the excitement of novelty and adventure (including some hot new sexual prospects) than on the safety of Mom and Dad. Survival and success were more likely when traveling with a crew.

Teenager behavior and attitudes have played an important role in the survival of the species. So teenagers are going to act like teenagers.

The toddler was a preview of teenage coming attractions

Remember when you had a sweet, fat baby who would nap in your arms? Then they became a toddler? A three-foot-tall sociopathic caveman began charging through your home, throwing fits and breaking shit. It is fortunate for them that they were also super cute little cave people, so we kept them. Evolution planned this well. If destruction and chaos follow you, it is best to be supercute. Why else would anyone ever get a puppy?

About ten years post-toddler, you have a teenager. Toddlers and teenagers alike are going through periods of significant brain development and reorganizing. These periods can be rough and messy. Like werewolf transformations.

> *"You see us as you want to see us—in the simplest terms with the most convenient definitions."*
>
> —*THE BREAKFAST CLUB* (1985)

Toddlers are learning that they are separate beings from their parents. They are practicing being separate from you. They run away from where they are supposed to be while yelling "NO!" As toddlers grow and get used to their physical autonomy, things settle down. For about ten years.

Teenagers are transitioning from being dependent children into being independent adults. So they pull away. Like toddlers, teenagers push boundaries and experiment with being separate from you. Rather than behave like little cavemen, they may act skeptical, critical, judgmental, and even contemptuous of you. To see some humor in the situation, catch the *South Park* episode "Help, My Teenager Hates Me!" (Season 25, Episode 5). In my favorite scene, Cartman says, "All he does is talk about his miserable life. I'm like, okay, Dude, I've got problems, too. But of course teenagers don't care about your problems. Look Buddy, I live in a hotdog."

Recall the moody, self-centered toddler? Toddlers have nothing on teenagers when it comes to being moody and self-centered. It is nice that the teenager can drink out of a cup without soaking themselves and that they know what happens when they pull on the Christmas tree branches. However, that cup they mastered as a toddler? It may be back on the table, but now red and filled with cheap vodka.

Science. Brain development. Evolution. All more interesting if you aren't outside chain-smoking, worrying about what the hell your darling is up to out there in the world. (Yep, I've done that. If it wouldn't make me sick and poisoned, and I could find a decent place to sit, I'd do it now just for fun.) Having a teenager in the house is potentially crazy-making, but less so when you realize it isn't actually a coordinated plot against your sanity.

Of course you want your teenager to return your love in

an easily recognizable way. Like they did when they were little. However, they are not little anymore, and they have developmental jobs of higher priority than making you feel loved. When they do something thoughtful or loving to you, hang on to it, write it in your journal, appreciate it. DO NOT expect it.

CHAPTER 2: SLEEP

I'll Get You a Mockingbird If You Go to Sleep

Why a chapter about sleep? This isn't a book about physical health, and duh, we know people need sleep, is this really chapter-worthy? Yes. This whole book is stuff that isn't talked about enough, and therefore teenagers getting enough sleep is on-brand here.

More oversimplified science: PreFrontalCortex, Dopamine, EasilyBored, ThrillSeeker, Impulsive, HighEmotions, and Amorous are hanging out, and the only one in the gang prone to suggesting "Let's Think" is PreFrontalCortex. You know what makes parents' best friend, PreFrontalCortex, stronger? Sleep. You know what makes PreFrontalCortex weaker? Lack of sleep.

How well do you manage whatever it is you are supposed to be managing when you are sleep deprived? For most of us it isn't pretty. You are a grown-ass adult with a fully developed prefrontal cortex and some life experience behind you. And you are in good company if you are on edge, bitchy, emotional, or apparently stupid when you are sleep deprived. How easy was your toddler to deal with when they were short on sleep? You had a three-foot-tall crazy (crazier) person on your hands. Sleep deprivation is no bueno. It is even more no bueno for a teenager.

PreFrontalCortex needs sleep—a lot of it

The American Academy of Sleep Medicine recommends that teens sleep eight to ten hours a night. We've already addressed PreFrontalCortex not being fully on the job in your darling's head. PreFrontalCortex develops and connects to the rest of the brain during sleep. The PreFrontalCortex refrain "Let's Think" gets stronger during sleep. When tired, there's a good chance PreFrontalCortex hears what the other characters are plotting and decides, "I just can't right now with these idiots. I'm too tired."

The Teenage Brain, by Frances E. Jensen, MD, takes a deep dive into teenage brain circuit development. An understanding of the physical development of a teenager's brain and that development's impact on their behaviors and attitudes will make teenagers less dumbfounding to the rest of us. "So what happens when teenagers don't get enough sleep? Nothing good, that's for sure," according to Dr. Jensen. "There is not a single part of a teenager's life that is not adversely affected by a lack of sleep."[2]

Good stuff happens during sleep: Short-term knowledge moves to long-term knowledge (learning efficiency), creativity and insight connections get made, the body heals and grows, and the hormones that control hunger are kept in balance.

---

[2] Frances E. Jensen and Amy E. Nutt, *The Teenage Brain* (HarperCollins, 2015), 96.

I've gotten militant about my own sleep after reading *Why We Sleep*, by Matthew Walker, PhD. Walker takes his reader through all the brain-health maintenance that occurs during sleep.

Just say no to sleep deprivation

Some high achievers of the past have boasted about getting by on just a few hours of sleep a night. Margaret Thatcher, Ronald Reagan, and Thomas Edison (cocaine was involved with this one) reputedly slept only about four hours a night. Getting by on less sleep was a popular goal several years ago. There was a book advocating getting yourself a great life by sleeping four hours a night and taking catnaps in toilet stalls during the day. (Yes, really.) I would love to need less sleep. However…once upon a time cigarettes were advertised as being good for you. Now only a crazy person would boast about smoking a pack a day. We may want sleep deprivation and cigarettes to be good for us, but that does not make it so.

The problems caused, or at least exacerbated, by teenagers not getting enough sleep should be all over the zeitgeist. The particular grimness of teenage mental health statistics gets plenty of attention. Here are just a couple of recent titles from a three-minute Google search: "Why American Teens Are So Sad," *The Atlantic*, Derek Thompson, April 2022; and "'It's Life or Death': The Mental Health Crisis Among U.S. Teens," *The New York Times*, Matt Richtel, April 2022. Social media, isolation, and parental high expectations regularly get listed as factors. Sleep deprivation is also a contributing factor to this mess, and it doesn't get talked about nearly enough.

Sleep deficiency charges up the excitability of that character HighEmotions. Walker describes the following, related to a study, in *Why We Sleep*: "In a flash, sleep deprived subjects (adult) would go from being irritable and antsy to punch-drunk giddy, only to then swing back to a state of vicious negativity. They were traversing enormous emotional distances, from negative to neutral to positive, and all the way back again, within a remarkably short period of time."[3] Wider and faster emotional swings, from a person without a fully wired prefrontal cortex, is exactly what we don't need around the house.

There are sleep adversaries

It doesn't seem like sleep should be all that difficult; this should be an easy part of parenting. And yet this is the chapter of the book where I make some suggestions that sound like micromanaging. Sleep has some mighty adversaries. Nature. Nature tends to be quite powerful. Real Life. How many times does Real Life thwart our plans? Screens. You know how powerful screens are.

Sleep Adversary One: Nature, presenting as Circadian Rhythm. There are people who say, "It's already 10:00 p.m." and those who say, "It's only 10:00 p.m." Teenagers are "It's only 10:00 p.m." people. Circadian rhythm, responsible for our cycles of sleep and wakefulness, decided at some point

> "Whatever you do, don't fall asleep."
>
> —A NIGHTMARE ON ELM STREET (1984)

---

3   Matthew Walker, *Why We Sleep: Unlocking the Power of Sleep and Dreams* (Scribner, 2017), 147.

that teenagers would be night owls and find it physically difficult to go to sleep early, even when they are expected to get up early in the morning. There are theories related to why Sir Circadian decided on this schedule for teenagers, one of which is that by staying up later than their parents, they are beginning the process of disconnecting from parental supervision. But who cares? What matters here is that the teenager being an "It's only 10:00 p.m." person is part of their physical development.

Sleep Adversary Two: Real Life. Walker sums up the challenge: "Neither society nor our parental attitudes are well designed to appreciate or accept that teenagers need more sleep than adults, and that they are biologically wired to obtain that sleep at a different time from their parents."[4]

School boards have fallen short in considering sleep requirements. Walker writes, "Forced by the hand of early school start times, this state of chronic sleep deprivation is especially concerning considering that adolescence is the most susceptible phase of life for developing chronic mental illnesses, such as depression, anxiety, schizophrenia, and suicidality."[5]

A paper published by the Journal of School Health reviewed thirty-eight reports examining the association between school start times, sleep, and other outcomes among adolescent students. "Most studies reviewed provide evidence that delaying school start time increases weeknight sleep duration among adolescents, primarily by delaying rise times. Most of the studies saw a significant increase in sleep duration even with relatively small delays in start times of

---

[4] Walker, *Why We Sleep*, 92.

[5] Walker, *Why We Sleep*, 308.

half an hour or so. Later start times also generally correspond to improved attendance, less tardiness, less falling asleep in class, better grades, and fewer motor vehicle crashes."[6] Those are obviously good things.

Making school start times later is an obvious first step in getting these kids more sleep. You, however, may not be able to get school start times changed just because you said so. I am 100 percent a fan of you becoming an advocate of change, even a real pain in the ass, with your local school board. For a deeper dive into addressing teens and sleep, particularly on how to work with school boards, I recommend *The Sleep-Deprived Teen*, by Lisa L. Lewis, MS.

Sleep Adversary Three: Screens. For millennia teenage humans have been night owls, and it seems to have been fine. This third adversary is only a couple of decades old, but oh so strong. Screens are more than happy to keep us up into the night, beyond when we would naturally have gone to sleep. Brilliant people design apps, games, and content to keep us at the screen, awake. We are of no value to advertisers, and therefore apps, when we are asleep. I know grown-ass adults who have to keep their phone away from their bed because they know what can happen. You think you can do just a bit of Instagram scrolling before shut-eye, but then that turns into an hour or more (in my case, videos of bulldogs). Tim Ferris calls this battle taking a knife to a gunfight.

Screens are the largest nemesis of sleep. Screen use and its impact on our lives at all ages deserves consideration, and there is plenty of information "out there." *Behind Their*

---

6   Anne G. Wheaton et al., "School Start Times, Sleep, Behavioral, Health, and Academic Outcomes: A Review of the Literature," *Journal of School Health* 86, no. 5 (2016): 363, https://doi.org/10.1111/josh.12388.

Screens—What Teens Are Facing and Adults Are Missing, by Emily Weinstein and Carrie James, describes very well the complexities and nuances of social media, sexting, and peer dynamics. Here, let's address just the sleep nemesis aspect.

Screens have another power over teenagers. Peer relationships are of paramount importance to this age group. Social media and gaming are where large parts of these relationships are playing out. A threat to a teenager's screen time is a threat to their relationships—relationships they are more than happy to fight the likes of you to protect. Screens and peer relationships put Sir Circadian and Real Life to shame.

Let's take all of the above and conclude that your darling would likely be better served with more sleep than they are getting. Encouraging and protecting your kid's sleep will require effort, some of which will be unpleasant and inconvenient. The adversaries are real. You, Dear Reader, may not know this yet, but you soon will. I am no fan of micromanagement. Kids figure stuff out when given the opportunity. Teenagers are interns at life, and interns learn by doing. However, *sleep is too important to be left completely up to an intern.*

Sleep *should* be an easy sell

Throwing rules at teenagers is a suboptimal first approach. And yet, sleep is SO IMPORTANT. So before making any sudden moves, you need to get some buy-in from your darling. First, *sell* sleep:

1. Sleep makes you less likely to get sick. If you do get sick, sleep helps you get well faster. You miss out on stuff when you are sick.

2. Whatever your thing is, sports particularly, sleep makes you better. Not only are injuries less likely, but injuries heal faster. If you are playing a sport, you probably want to be good at it.
3. Sleep makes you look better.
4. Sleep makes you less likely to eat too much crappy food and feel unhealthy.
5. Sleep makes you smarter and able to get better grades with less effort. Even if you could give two shits about grades, easier seems like a good thing.
6. Sleep helps you keep your emotions from overtaking you. You'll feel less angry at other people and better able to not let other people get to you. You'll feel less anxious and less depressed.

The case for sleep is an easy sell. But the adversaries are worthy—especially screens. Shutting down the screens to get more sleep will not seem as obvious a first move to your kid. (Remember, these people took a bit longer than adults to determine that setting their hair on fire was a bad idea.)

I advocate for screens to be off by ten o'clock on school nights. This is where parent overlordship has clear value. If a kid's parents make it difficult for the kid to be texting or scrolling on social media after ten o'clock, then it isn't the kid's fault if they aren't available to their peers. A real friend or decent paramour can wait until morning to be in touch.

Of course you'll get this objection: "But I have homework…" Your kid is smart and knows you care about grades. I submit to the court that sleep is more important than grades. Homework is going to need to be done before ten o'clock, or they'll have to use paper. Yep, they'll have to plan ahead, and they probably won't like it. If your darling says they aren't tired, that's fine, there's paper. Read, write, draw, paint. On paper.

Use technology against itself. Phone functionality and Wi-Fi access can be managed now, and more solutions are being created. As of this writing, phones on an Apple Family plan can be restricted by a controlling phone. There are also Yondr bags. A phone goes into the Yondr bag, and the bag can only be opened with a special device. Sleep is important enough to be *THAT* parent whose rules are *SO unreasonable and out of touch*.

Don't wake the teenager!

It will be much easier to keep them asleep than to get them to go to sleep. Support your darling sleeping as late as possible, given the demands of real life.

Facilitate your darling sleeping as late as possible and still getting to school on time. If driving them to school will save time compared to having them take the bus, and you can, put on your chauffeur cap and get at it. Embrace any morning routine that gets them from bed to out-the-door as quickly as possible.

Suggest that, the night before, they set out everything that is to be taken with them in the morning. Do this yourself and occasionally comment on why you do it—less anxiety in the morning, less risk of forgetting something that creates a time waste, and so on. More sleep may be motivation enough for them. However, your kid may conclude you are way too uptight. You might as well prepare for "the look" from them: the one indicating you have no idea what you are talking about.

Provide reasonably healthy breakfasts meant for on-the-run consumption. Protein smoothie. Overnight oats. Peanut butter and jelly sandwich. Bagel and cream cheese. Sausage and egg sandwich. Run them through McDonald's for an Egg McMuffin on the way to school. There are many options. Your mission is morning speed.

Your kid may have a superstar look to maintain every morning. The hair. The makeup. Beauty takes time. You may cut some time from the process by finding a hair and makeup person to suggest how to look cool and correct in the shortest amount of time. There's got to be someone on YouTube doing this sort of thing.

Many morning commitments are set by school, sports, or clubs. Discourage early morning jobs in favor of afternoon or evening shifts. Let the elders take the early Starbucks shifts. When the outside world isn't demanding that your kid show up in the morning, don't wake them up. Let them sleep.

Letting them sleep in should go over well, just like buying them stuff does. They'll be nice to you. They want to sleep, just not necessarily when you want them to sleep.

Going forward I won't be advocating for a lot of micromanagement or control-freakishness. This chapter could easily have given you the wrong idea about me.

> *"How'd you like to spend the next several nights wondering if your crazy out-of-work bum uncle will shave your head while you sleep? See you in the car."*
>
> *—UNCLE BUCK (1989)*

CHAPTER 3: APPEARANCES

Large Child? No. More Beautiful Adult? Not that either

When your darling acts like a petulant child, it is easy to treat them as you would a large child. When they are big enough to be a more beautiful adult, it is easy to think they are adult-capable at decision-making. There is a balance between not going too far toward treating a teenager as a large child and not going too far the other way and treating them as a more beautiful adult. My temptation is to say, "It's hard. Good luck!" and end the chapter. But that's not my way. So, Dear Parent, let's do this.

If you view teenagers as large children, you may try to have Amazon send you breathable child bubble wrap to protect them. Or maybe someone on Etsy can send you a

> "But, as you well know, appearances can be deceiving."
>
> —THE MATRIX RELOADED (2003)

parachute, enabling you to drop in as some sort of superhero and save every day. Your kid is precious; of course you'd like bubble wrap and a parachute. We protect and care for what we love. Here's the rough part: It's time to start letting them practice problem-solving and resilience, both of which are learned on the job of life.

Teenagers typically perceive themselves to be new adults, so if you talk to them like they are large children, you are going to annoy them. (Annoying people have less influence on others.) Your speaking tone won't match their self-perception, and they may tune you out or avoid speaking with you. That is the opposite of what you want.

At the other end of the spectrum, you may treat them like more beautiful adults. That's what they look like. That's what they think they are.

They look like more beautiful adults, but they aren't

Teenagers can navigate cities, get driver's licenses, and learn SO much so fast. They can be physically strong and undeniably beautiful. They can sing and dance and play sports better than most adults. Whether or not they admit it, they can clean a house, mow a lawn, and do laundry.

Just because they can feed themselves, it is easy to think that it is fine for them to not have adults around in the evenings and on the weekends and that you can just let them be. Give some thought to the cafeteria table of characters before leaving for the weekend. PreFrontalCortex is not to be counted on. When your kid is five, you know they shouldn't be left alone because their skills and judgment aren't there. (Ironically, the fourteen-year-old is the one more likely to be playing with fire or screwing around on the roof.)

When you are fourteen, you don't know you are fourteen. On vacation, my fourteen-year-old self and my best friend absolutely could not understand why my mom wouldn't let us go to the disco with the cute eighteen-year-old boys we'd met at the pool.

I asked a young adult woman whether, when she was a teenager, she had known she was in situations she shouldn't have been in. She answered, "No, I thought I was, like, forty."

It's easy to lean one way or the other

Some parents treat their kids like they need a parent's help with everything. Some go the other direction and assume their kids can handle any situations or decisions. There are those who manage to go all-in on both. Ask a teacher at an affluent high school: Do the same parents who argue with teachers and coaches on behalf of their kid also put their sixteen-year-old in a sports car? The answer is often yes.

Your darlings were actual children, like yesterday, right? You probably mastered the hell out of being a grade-school parent. You continue to want to protect your darling from failure and bad days. Of course you do. However, unless you feed and house your kid forever, and they never get a job, or fall in love, or take on a goal, you can't protect them from failure and bad days. There are furniture corner covers to protect toddlers from tables. There is no version you can order from the nice people at Amazon to protect your teenager from heartbreak and disappointment.

You know life occasionally punches people in the face. You want your kid to learn to take a hit while you are still around to support them in learning how. While I am no fan of bull riding, there is a process to becoming a bull rider. An aspiring bull rider doesn't start by hopping onto a bull. They start as kids getting thrown off sheep and calves. They land in the animal shit and get up and out of the way, over and over. Later, when a very large and justifiably pissed-off bull named MoFo sends them flying, they'll have practiced getting the hell away from the likes of MoFo. While a kid can be hurt by a sheep or a calf, they are unlikely to be permanently damaged or killed. MoFo can be a different story.

The parental goal is to let them learn, unfortunately via practice, the resilience required to deal with bad days and disappointments. And simultaneously keep them out of the ER.

They are not large children

There are a couple of common ways to treat a teenager like a large child. One, talk to them as you would talk to a young child, thereby infantilizing and totally annoying them. Two, take on their problems as "we" problems. HBO provides an egregious two-for-one example.

The HBO documentary *Addiction* includes a woman bringing her daughter home from rehab. While the daughter is twenty-three, the following would be as inappropriate were the daughter sixteen. The mother seems like a good person who obviously loves her daughter. But she treats her daughter like a young child.

When the daughter doesn't respond to some rando third

> *"With certain obvious exceptions, werewolves are people, just like anyone else."*
>
> —TEEN WOLF (1985)

person, the mother says to her *twenty-three-year-old* daughter, "What do you say?" in *that* tone. The one you use with a preschooler to remind them about "please" and "thank you." Then the mother tousles her *twenty-three-year-old*'s hair. When you speak to someone like they are a child, you lose credibility with them. Because you are *annoying*. You will also sound like you think they are a child, which is insulting on top of being annoying. Repeat from above: You most want your kid to talk to you. So your first step is to try not to be annoying or insulting.

Beyond annoying all of us with the above vignette, the mother is taking on her daughter's situation as a "WE" project. The mother tells us, "Sometimes I think I'm not going to make it. But then I turn around and say I have to make it. I mean, she's all I have. If anything happens to me, then she won't make it. And I want *her* to make it. 'Cause I believe in her. I know she can make it."

Wait, what? There is the glaring contradiction of the mother saying she believes in her daughter, but only if the daughter has her. Of course this young woman can make it. We don't know whether she will or not or even exactly what "make it" means, but she can make it without her mother.

People are capable of incredible things. This is true of your kid, whether or not they act like it.

There is more from the mother that makes me frown and tilt my head like a confused dog: "Gonna run the house like a rehab." "We need to sit down and make a plan, a goal, a contract, something, and live by it. That sound good?" "You help me and I'll help you, and maybe we'll make it."

Maybe? We'll?

You can keep your kid's challenges from becoming "we" projects while still being there to support them as they figure things out. Start by questioning yourself anytime you are about to say "we" regarding an issue. Show your kid some respect by not taking on their life, challenges, or accomplishments as "we" projects. Let them own their wins and their hot messes. Being in your kid's corner, which is a parent's job forever, is different from taking on their problems as "we" problems.

The abovementioned mother would have sounded more helpful, and respectful, if she'd said something like the following: "I know so much sucks right now. I want you to tell me how I can help." "Tell me what you need, even if what you need is for me to shut up." "I'm happy to just listen." "If you want to, let's go walk, or drive around, or peruse the bookstore." "I'll do whatever." "I'm here."

When you make your kid's project a "we" project, you are treating them as incapable. You are basically saying, "You will 100 percent fuck this up if I don't do it for you." No bueno.

Don't try to be a Ray Donovan fixer

Guiding and supporting do not require you to take ownership of their problems. You can support your kid by listening to them and strategizing with them about *their challenge*. Guiding and supporting without taking ownership (attempting to take control) can be frightfully difficult because your darling may be in a terrifying circumstance.

Have their back without taking control and putting their responsibilities onto yourself. You would be in good company were you to attempt to alleviate your own anxiety (terror) by trying to take over and control the situation. I'm so sorry, but you can't control the situation, at least not in a sustainable way. Use your own support network to support you while you support your kid.

Your young, amazing superhuman, because they are human, will probably fuck up. They may get bested and beat. They may get dumped. It HURTS when your kid hurts. However, Dear Parent, you will suck it up, love them and support them, and guide *them* in dealing with whatever punch *they've* taken.

Confidence and resilience are developed. Pride is earned by doing difficult things. We can't buy pride or visualize it into existence. We must earn it. What more do you want than for your kid to launch into the world with confidence, resilience, and pride? This stuff is learned on the job of life by overcoming challenges and setbacks. It won't always be puppies and unicorns. If a butterfly is helped out of the cocoon, rather than allowed to struggle its way out, it won't develop the strength required to fly. Butterflies are beautiful, but becoming one isn't.

Cautionary tale regarding Ray Donovan parenting: It is currently not uncommon for people to bring their parents to job interviews. Human Resource departments get calls from the *PARENTS* of working *ADULTS* who are struggling at work. More than a few HR people wish I were making that up.

You can (and should) put up guardrails

PreFrontalCortex is on the scene sometimes but is not to be counted on. The self-perception of a teenager is likely "I know what I'm doing." Maybe. But also maybe not. What would be helpful? Parents. (That's you.) What else would be helpful? Guardrails. (Your darling probably won't agree.)

Guardrails reduce opportunities for your kid to make unfortunate choices or get into situations they aren't ready for.

Curfew Guardrail. A parent may assume their kid's decision-making is as good at 2 a.m. as it is at 11 p.m. None of ours is. Assume nothing good happens after midnight and have a midnight curfew.

Post-Event Guardrail. When you pick up your kid after a dance/party/concert yourself, you don't have to worry about post-event parties with randos up to God knows what. Pick your kid up from the concert. The concert may end after your bedtime. Drink coffee.

Safety-Most-Important Guardrail. Make it crystal clear to your kid, over and over, that you are to be called anytime to come get them from anywhere for any reason. (This directive will be repeated in this book because I like it so much.) No questions should be asked of them other than "Are you all right? Do you need anything?" This minimizes the risk that after a stupid choice, a more stupid one gets made in order to not get in trouble for the first one. Like drinking and then driving. Or riding with someone who has been drinking. *The Teenage Brain*, by Francis E. Jensen, MD, includes a story of a boy who got lost walking home in a snowstorm. He hid from passing cars because he didn't want to get in trouble for drinking. He ended up in the hospital after being found nearly frozen to death.

Be-Around Guardrail. Don't leave them home alone for a night or a weekend and assume they'll handle the freedom and empty house the way you would like them to. In addition to party hosting potential, the curfew guardrail comes off the table. Be home so that when they come home, you can say, "I'm glad you're home."

The argument against guardrails is obvious; it's too easy. Sex and drugs and drinking and dangerous mayhem can take place anywhere, anytime. True, true, and true. Real guardrails don't stop all cars from careening into disaster. One, guardrails can't be everywhere. Two, a car can hit something else or go so fast that it bombs right over the guardrail. Guardrails exist to make terrible accidents less likely.

Maybe you don't think your kid will do stupid shit. They may not. But they may. Or someone in their crew may. Guardrails aren't put up just to protect us from our own driving. They are also there to protect us from bad driving and mistakes made by other drivers.

NO ONE HAS TO LIKE IT. Guardrails are unlikely to be met with "Thanks, Dad. I didn't think about it like that" à la *The Brady Bunch*. More likely, they will bitch and moan about the unfairness and whatever *EVERYONE* else gets to do and all the things they are missing. Explain to your darling that it isn't personal; you are just doing your job. Their job description may include bitching and moaning. It's fine.

An aside about sports cars

As mentioned, affluent parents often give teenagers sports cars. Don't give a teenager a sports car. A clunker, that's what they should get. They can do less damage with it. Reliable would be nice, but ugly is fine. I don't care if you are wealthy (Go You!) or your kid goes to an affluent high school. Your kid does not need a fast, powerful car. Of course they want one.

I want one. They are beautiful and go vroom vroom. Yes, you would like to be parent hero of the day and buy them one and see how happy they are and how much they love you that day. Don't do it. A sports car can go really fast, and driving recklessly is fun. Racing is fun. They may try this nonsense in a 2005 Honda Civic. But not well.

Of course it isn't easy. So, yes, Dear Parent, some of the above sounds contradictory. Overprotective: no bueno. Overpermissive: no bueno. However, you've been here before. Your kid learned to ride a bike, and not by riding in the basket of yours. They fell and skinned their elbows and knees and cried. While you didn't like it, you sucked it up and let it happen. You also put a helmet on them and kept them out of traffic. The idea was that, yes, they could get hurt. But not *TOO* hurt.

PART TWO

The Emotions

I ran into a good explanation of emotional needs at a yard sale. I paid five dollars for a set of Tony Robbins's CDs. An infomercial-watching insomniac must have ordered them at some point.

While there are credentialed psychologists who give Tony Robbins grief for not being one of them, whatever, I don't really care. What he says makes sense to me. Robbins identifies six emotional needs motivating behavior and each choice we make as an attempt to meet one or more of these needs.

The wise parent deliberately supports and prioritizes three of those needs at home: Stability, Importance, and Connection. These needs make up the next few chapters. As for the remaining emotional needs identified by Robbins—Uncertainty, Growth, and Contribution—you won't hear this often from me, but parents get free passes on these three:

Uncertainty. These easily bored darlings seek novelty and adventure without you.

Growth. Teenagers are growing, with or without you, whether you or they like it or not.

Contribution. Contribution is usually an older person's game, but if your kid becomes so inclined, they'll find volunteer opportunities or just unload the dishwasher without being asked.

Enjoy the free passes; there aren't many.

This section is not about embroidering a sampler or hanging a "Live, Laugh, Love" sign in your kitchen. Your darling's choices out there in the world will be influenced by your relationship with them and how okay they feel. Relationships and feeling okay have the same components (as in met needs).

You can make your kid feel safe, and important, and connected, and therefore less likely to go looking for those feelings in all the wrong places. If the needs for Stability,

Importance, and Connection are met at home, your kid heads out the door and into Peer World wanting more but not needing more.

CHAPTER 4: STABILITY

Terra Firma

Certainty is predictable. We know we like certainty, because Starbucks is everywhere. We order our drink of choice knowing exactly what we are going to get. We get a small predictable moment in the day. Dolly Parton may have poured herself a cup of ambition; now Starbucks pours us cups of certainty.

A well-run preschool demonstrates the power of predictability. Short cavepeople move from activity to activity throughout the day knowing what to expect next. Toddlers—*TODDLERS*—appear calm and reasonable.

Your kid should know what they are going to get in their home. While there are about a million people online to teach you how to have a well-managed, decluttered, spotless home, you, Dear Parent, are the most important part of your kid's home.

"Home Sweet Home" matters

Recall that kid, PreFrontalCortex, introduced in Chapter 1. Recall that PreFrontalCortex is underdeveloped and easily ignored by Yoda-strength Dopamine. PreFrontalCortex is responsible for thinking things through and regulating thoughts, emotions, and impulses. PreFrontalCortex is the kid who considers risk and consequences. PreFrontalCortex is at their best in a stable home environment.

If you Google "stress and the adolescent brain," you can go down a deep rabbit hole of scientific studies. If scientific papers aren't your jam, this is what you need to know: Not only does short-term stress impair the immediate functioning of PreFrontalCortex, but long-term chronic stress can prevent some of the important connections to the rest of the brain from forming to begin with. You want PreFrontalCortex to have the best chance at catching a break and being heard at the cafeteria table of characters living in your kid's head.

Maybe a kid appears not to care one way or the other if the parental unit shows up late, or drunk, or distracted. This is unlikely to be true. However, they will adapt and not set themselves up to be disappointed by you. The TV show *Shameless* provides an extreme example. The kids have accepted and adapted to the drunkenness and fucked-up-ness of Frank, their dad. They treat Frank sort of like a stray dog that comes around. No one questions when he will be home. No one goes to him for support. They show no sign of caring whether Frank is happy to see them or not.

> "This is my house. I have to defend it."
>
> —HOME ALONE (1990)

Have your own shit together

If you are a hot mess, your kid will not count on you to be there for them. They will not look to you for support and guidance.

Amazon can send you books advocating a parental control grab (there are several). Many of these books sing about "reestablishing authority" and stop just short of encouraging you to beat your chest. As much as I love gorillas, please don't do this. Many authors presume your teenager is your adversary, and chapter after chapter instructs you how to grab control and win the day. However, even the most annoying of these books includes a nod toward getting your own shit together in order to effectively parent.

I'm paraphrasing, of course; other authors tend to be much more polite. Family problems such as alcohol or drug abuse, mental illness or depression, and marital or divorce issues are presented as impairing your ability to get your kid "under control." I say let's step back: The family problems are potentially (probably) contributing to the kid making subpar choices in order to alleviate their own stress at home. People's behavior generally isn't random. People, including your kids, adapt to their circumstances in order to meet their needs, sometimes in maladaptive ways.

You know if you are unhappy, resentful, regularly in tears of despair or rage, and spending as much time avoiding your life as possible. Your 100-percent-not-stupid kid will know it too. Hot-mess parents tend to have anxious, stressed, or lonely kids who haven't gotten enough life under their belts to know that their feelings are rooted in the environment they inhabit rather than their own shortcomings. The kid will feel anxious and stressed at home without necessarily knowing why. A family is an interrelated ecosystem. Everyone is impacted by the state of everyone else in the family. If you are an emotional mess, get help. Your getting emotionally stable is as much a parenting responsibility as is making sure they have food. There are books and podcasts and journals and therapists. Get what you can. Do what you can.

Obviously if someone is struggling with depression, trauma, or grief, this is a bigger topic than can be addressed in a few paragraphs saying, "Get your shit together." People struggling emotionally aren't struggling just because they have neglected to get their shit together. I have been the emotionally unreliable mother. I *KNOW* this struggle is not solved by a paragraph or two in any book or even several books. There are resources and people out there who are actually qualified (to be crystal clear, I am not) to address emotional hot messes.

Maybe you should talk to someone

Pharma solutions can be polarizing and are not always effective. I propose that even if you see pharma solutions as shortcuts and Band-Aids on trauma and grief, maybe that's okay while you have a kid to raise. Life can be a real bitch. You may fear IRS Dobermans or some other types of unpleasant wolves at the door. You may feel bad about yourself as a professional failure or feel fat or old. You may simply be heartbroken.

Be vigilant about not unloading your problems on your kid any more than you would (or at least should) at work. You do not want your kid avoiding you like everyone in the office avoids the office self-appointed victim of all slights and injustices. It is not your darling's job to keep you company or listen to you. They are not around for you. You are to be around for them. What you need to do for yourself you can do on your own time. Any of your stress-induced rants are for close adult friends and paid therapists and your dog.

If drugs or alcohol (alcohol is a drug, people—it's called out separately due to its rampant popularity) are causing problems for you or your family, then drugs or alcohol are a problem you are responsible for addressing. As with other emotional struggles, getting your shit together with drugs or alcohol is WAY easier said than done. However, it is your responsibility as a parent to get what help and support you can and do what you can to minimize the impact any drugs or alcohol are having on your family. Also, I'll assume that someone along the way has informed you that what you model to your kids is way more influential than what you say to them.

True story: Kim's (name changed to protect the innocent) parents were drug and alcohol chaos and destruction enthusiasts. There were ugly years in her home while she was growing up. One night Kim's teenage son got drunk and was brought home by friends and poured through the front door. Kim's husband, Jim (real name), lost his shit and blamed this scene on the curse of Kim's fucked-up family. Kim responded, "Then why is he smoking your brand of cigarettes and drinking your brand of beer?" (I love her.) The drunk kid on the couch yelled, "Yeah, Dad!" (I love that kid too.)

> "Welcome to our home. There's a belfry, a swamp, and a dungeon down below."
>
> —ADDAMS FAMILY VALUES (1993)

It is okay to expect politeness

I am big on manners. The old-fashioned Emily Post kind. I like peace and order. Manners and assumptions of mutual respect contribute to Terra Firma. An environment is more predictable (read: stable) when the people present know what to reasonably expect from each other.

Aside and also, one responsibility of parenting is to launch a likable person other people want to be around and support. Manners make people likable.

These have been my expectations of my kids and myself:

We are polite:

> You don't have to like me, love me, or like or love anything I say. However, you are to be polite. We don't yell at each other, interrupt one another, or look at a screen while one of us is speaking to the other.

> We say please and thank you.

> We eat with our mouths closed.

> We respond politely with clear voices to hellos and questions from servers, store clerks, and adult family members and family friends.

> We do not start eating until the person who prepared the meal sits down, unless they tell us to go ahead.

> If your room is a pigsty, fine; you live in it. If the smell or the crap makes it into the hallway, you will have to handle it.

Whatever responsibilities you have around the house are to be done before you leave, not "When I get home."

If you do something half-assed, you'll get to fix it. (My daughter once put the lid on the garbage can half-assed and then left town for a week. The crows had a party. I took a picture of the holy mess and sent it to her. She said, "I'm sorry." I said, "It's not a big deal. You can clean it up when you get home." So I left it as it was, and of course it got worse over the week, and it was there for her to clean up when she got home. The neighbors probably weren't fans of my "logical consequence" parenting, but whatever. I live in Seattle; I have no idea what their names were.)

Because I am still responsible for you and I feed you, I get some privileges:

> I will decide on curfews, activities you are not allowed to attend, and those you may attend if I pick you up from them.

> Curfew is only negotiable before it is set. For every minute you are late for curfew, your next curfew will be shortened by five minutes, and I'll decide when this time debt gets applied. Being on time shows consideration for the person waiting for you. I expect that consideration.

I have responsibilities:

> I do my best to communicate clearly. I will make statements such as "Curfew is eleven o'clock," not "Curfew is eleven o'clock, okay?"

I don't apologize for parenting, or facts, or expectations.

I will tell you what I want you to do around the house with plenty of notice and time for you to get it handled. I won't surprise you with a last-minute "You need to do X now."

I want to hear, and will consider, your perspective.

This is what you get:

While your actions have consequences in the outside world, I won't add to any of the consequences you incur for some stupidness done outside our home. Consequences from the outside world stand alone.

Because I am your parent and not your friend, I will never not love you. I will always be there for you, even if I must sign in at a prison. For the rest of my life, as much as I possibly can, when you need me, I will come.

Be on time

Being on time is a manner that tends to be underrated. Being on time makes you predictable, which creates stability. (It also shows people you are important to them.) Be where you say you will be when you say you will be there. Your kid would like to not have to guess when you are going to show up, whatever the circumstances. I used to be an often-late person. As an introvert, I identify with the sweatshirt that says, "I'm sorry I'm late. I didn't really want to come." Your lateness can feel to the person waiting like you didn't really want to come, whether or not it's true. You don't want your kid to think you didn't want to show up.

I stopped being late when I decided being on time was important, particularly when one of my kids is involved. Some Oprah guru or Oprah herself has stated, "Nothing happens until you decide." Decide to be on time. You will then factor in commute time, plus buffer. You will start to enjoy being a bit early. Besides eliminating the running-late stress and apologies and excuses you need to come up with, you can enjoy some guilt-free Instagram. Now I will be on time to meet one of my kids even if I have to show up incorrectly dressed.

It's a bad look if you expect other people (like your kid) to be on time for things (like curfew) but you don't hold yourself to the same expectation. If you are vigilant about your kid's curfew, but you show up to stuff late, you've set yourself up to be called a hypocrite. Make your darling work to find a "You're a hypocrite" opportunity. Don't just give it to them.

CHAPTER 5: IMPORTANCE

They Want to Matter

By fostering Stability with your own emotional health, setting some expectations, and being where you say you will be when you say you will be there, you are also showing your kid that they are important to you.

Evidence that a kid feels significant to their caregivers and other important people in their lives isn't loud and flashy. There won't be a Guns N' Roses soundtrack to it. Look to logic. If people talk to people who listen to them, and if people feel important to people who listen to them, then people talk to people they feel important to. Therefore, if a kid is talking to you, they, at least in that moment, feel reasonably important to you. Well done, Dear Parent.

Feeling important feels like being recognized, appreciated, and respected. It feels like mattering. You want your kid to know *they matter to you*. Hard stop, with no qualifications or limitations.

Toddlers and preschoolers are obvious and loud about wanting attention from a parent. When a parent's attention is directed away from them and these small cavepeople don't approve of this misdirection of attention, they'll interrupt, start fights with each other, make demands, and throw fits. Attention communicates Importance. A young child probably isn't thinking this through: "I want proof that I'm important, so I want my parent to pay attention to me. Therefore, this is a good time to be a particularly annoying caveperson." Yet that's exactly what they do.

If young children choose antics to get attention, how do you know a teenager wants to be important to their parent? You have to assume. They probably aren't going to tell you. It's uncomfortable to tell someone that you don't feel important to them. Marriage counselors will attest to this. However, a teenager has likely mastered communicating "I don't care one way or the other." I submit to the court that this is never true.

Feeling important matters

You want your kid to feel important to you in order to increase the odds they will talk to you about fraught topics. You can see the challenge here. Whether or not your teenager feels important to you, you may not get clear or timely feedback from them. Your darling may act like they couldn't care less one way or the other. They may be snarky, dismissive, and aloof. None of this is relevant to your parenting. You do not need feedback. You do not need to be important to them.

> *"Do you think they are maybe the same thing? Love and attention?"*
>
> —LADY BIRD (2017)

Your job is to demonstrate beyond a reasonable doubt that your darling is IMPORTANT TO YOU.

If you sing about how important to you your darling is, then neglect to act like this is true, you'll look like a jerk. You don't show your kid they are important to you by singing their praises to them or to other people. Telling them and everyone else how special and brilliant and obviously gifted and impressive they are will not make them feel important to you. You may have experienced someone telling you that you are important to them and then acting in ways that make you feel unimportant. The person's actions, not their words, determined how you felt.

Aside: You also don't make them feel important to you by buying them unnecessary stuff. Although they will probably be really nice to you when you buy them stuff, everyone wants stuff, and your kid is not an idiot.

We often hear parents tell their kid, "I love you so much. You are the most important thing in the world to me." Then they pull something like one of the following: leaving the kid home alone so they can go out or go on a trip with friends, regularly hitting happy hour with friends or coworkers rather than being home to eat dinner with the kid, or continuing to watch a TV show or sports event when their kid walks into the room.

The human parent is unlikely to get 100 percent on this test

However, by being deliberate and attempting to get 100 percent, you are likely to hit 85 percent, which is pretty good, especially graded on a curve.

There are the obvious things you'll do. You will go to

their competitions and performances. Of course. That's the minimum. Are you around after the event to hear what they thought about it? Did you go to the game even when there was a social event of your own that evening?

Life happens and demands are made, and trying to appease everyone can be exhausting. There are loads of books and magazine articles promoting work/life balance and self-care, including the care and feeding of your adult relationships. I propose that "balance" is a moving target and that for the short period of your life when you have teenagers in the house, you should put availability to them at the top of your priority list and be more flexible with the rest. No life season is forever. You will eventually miss many parts of this one.

The average teenager has plenty of demands on their time. School, sports and clubs, and friends will all pull your kid out of the house. Do your self-care and adult relationships when your kid is busy elsewhere. When they are around, make being available to them your priority. They are going to launch soon, and then you are going to have more time than you know what to do with.

Rock star example

Dave Grohl, lead singer of the Foo Fighters, has demands and commitments. Probably more than you do. Once he had two concerts scheduled on the other side of the world. Tens of thousands of fans had bought tickets. He was committed. Between the two concerts was a father-daughter dance at home. During the brief time between the two concerts, he traveled hours and hours to get home to go to the dance for a couple hours and then flew back to the other side of the world in time for the next concert. He did that.

Now, the upside to being an actual rock star is the finances to make such things happen. Yet if you aren't an actual rock star, you probably don't have kazillion-dollar commitments on the other side of the world either. Be like Dave (except maybe not the outside-of-his-marriage-love-child part).

Ask questions, listen, and then listen some more

Know enough to have some specific questions. "How is X's hedgehog doing?" "What do you think of Y's boyfriend?" "Whose art in class is your favorite?" "I liked that teacher when I met them. What do you think?" These inquiries show you are paying attention to their world. Avoid questions that can be answered with a single word—like the most boring question ever, "How was school?" The goal of your questions is conversation, not interrogation. "What did you think about the test?" and "Was anyone surprised about what showed up on the test?" are better questions than "How did you do on the test?" Maybe (remember that you are dealing with a teenager—there are no guarantees) you'll score a conversation.

When your kid comes home, drop whatever you are doing or watching, and make it obvious they can have your full attention. If, out of nowhere, they start talking about *anything*, drop whatever you are doing and actively listen. Unless you are flying a plane, or on your air traffic controller shift, or in the courtroom, or in the operating room, or doing some

> *"I listened, but then I had a small piece of fluff in my ear. Could you say it again, please?"*
>
> —THE MANY ADVENTURES OF WINNIE THE POOH (1977)

other job where someone else's well-being is dependent upon you, stop whatever you are doing and listen to your kid. If you are tired, I don't care. Drink some coffee and listen to your kid. If you are worried about something, I don't care. Set it aside and listen to your kid. If you are air traffic controlling, make sure your kid knows when you will be available. Then be where you say you will be when you say you will be there. This *shows* your kid that they are important.

Listen to your kid as if they are talking about the most important thing in the world. Not because the topic is inherently important, but because your kid is.

In 1986, in a park in my hometown, a pregnant teenager was beaten to death by two or three teenage boys. The crew was led by a budding psychopath. Two girls in the crew went to the park and stayed away on a hill during the murder. In town several months later, I overheard two teenage girls talking in a neighboring restaurant booth. It became apparent that the girl speaking was one of the girls on the hill. Referring to the psychopath leader, she said, "but nobody listened to me the way he did." Do not raise a kid who can credit a psychopath murderer with listening to them better than you do.

An aside about divorce

Dear Parent, I would like this aside to not be for you. Not because I think you shouldn't get, or have gotten, divorced. I have no idea. But rather because divorce is hard on everyone. Divorce has the potential to take a wrecking ball to your kids feeling important.

I did my part to keep the divorce statistics up. My ex-husband and I, Ken and Redhead Barbie, married—without absolutely any idea how to do it well. So we didn't.

The well-being of everyone in a family is intertwined. Each individual in the family experiences the impact of a divorce differently, and each of them, in turn, also impacts the others. Marcus Aurelius summed it up: "What injures the hive, injures the bee." The potential for drama and discord and unhealthy coping strategies is exponential as a divorce plays out across the parties. If you are with the 50 percent of us who have pulled the divorce tab, triple-dog-double-double-down on the components of *showing* your kids how important they are to you.

In *Help at Any Cost*, Maia Szalavitz looked at "troubled-teen" programs. She wrote, "I was struck during my research for this book by how many times teens wound up in tough love programs in the midst or aftermath of a parental divorce."[7] It often appears the troubled-teen professionals will zero in on the behaviors of the troubled teens without considering the context of their lives. When a divorce turns a kid's world upside down, getting comfort and/or distraction is attractive, even if it's dangerous or destructive. People in pain seek relief—that's part of the human condition, not evidence of disease or of a bad kid.

I crossed paths with a fairly popular teen parenting book, *Parenting Teens with Love and Logic*, by Foster Cline and Jim Fay. The book was a bit churchy for me, but not terrible—until I got to the chapter on stepparenting and thought my head was going to blow off.

This is what these geniuses wrote: "The birth parent must make it absolutely clear to the children that her allegiance and love lies with her new husband—the person she will be spending the rest of her life with…it is a wise birth parent

---

7   Maia Szalavitz, *Help at Any Cost* (Riverhead Books, 2016), 230.

who lets the children know, unequivocally, that should family problems escalate, if anyone were to go, it would not be the new spouse."[8]

What? Are you kidding me? Second marriages fail even more than first marriages, and a parent's love and allegiance should be unconditionally with their kids, not someone who may or may not be around in ten years. Yes, I said it; the new partner may turn out to be a temp.

The Brady Bunch wasn't real. I wish it was. If you find an old rerun somewhere, you'll know it's not real because the backyard grass isn't real. Kids loved *The Brady Bunch* because the family looked like a great time. I'd love to have an Alice around to do all the work. I also want the not-up-to-current-building-code staircase. *The Brady Bunch*, like Disneyland and Las Vegas and Barbie, is a good time as long as you know it isn't real. If you watch *The Brady Bunch* and think that a stepfamily is going to be that happy and perfect from day one, you won't prepare for how much patience and love it is actually going to take. The stepparent situation is quite fraught.

A stepparent cannot come in swinging with rules and demands and taking priority over the kids. Everyone loses in power struggles. Discipline and rules should come from the original parent. This is the best shot at the kids and the new partner developing a good relationship over time. Before re-partnering up, the relationship between the new love interest and the kids needs to be allowed to develop naturally and possibly slowly. If this person really is "for the rest of your life," then eat some vegetables and get some exercise and there will be plenty of time for everyone to settle in with

---

[8] Foster Cline and Jim Fay, *Parenting Teens with Love and Logic* (Navigators, 2006), 144.

everyone else. The right partner has a vested interest in having a good relationship with your kids. Being your partner means doing right by your kids. Your kids are 100 percent for the rest of your life. The new partner, maybe.

The form of the family isn't what is important. What is important is that the adult(s) in the family prioritize the protection and raising of the young.

It isn't *The Brady Bunch*, even if fake grass is still a thing.

CHAPTER 6: CONNECTION

They Need Their People

Humans are social. We travel in packs. Our abilities to communicate and cooperate enabled us to become the apex predator, in spite of being physically pathetic among the animals. Pretty much everything can run away from us, and we are likewise easily caught. Our babies are born particularly helpless. We needed villages. The prehistoric people who did well in community with others survived. We are descendants of the well connected.

As it has been historically dangerous to the species for too many of us to be alone, loneliness hurts. Mother Nature wants us motivated to find our people. "Loneliness is far more than just a bad feeling...The mortality impact of being socially disconnected is similar to that caused by smoking up to fifteen cigarettes a day."[9] (There were years I smoked while lonely. That's unfortunate.)

---

9   Office of the Surgeon General, *Our Epidemic of Loneliness and Isolation: The U.S. Surgeon General's Advisory on the Healing Effects of Social Connection and Community* (US Department of Health and Human Services, 2023), 4.

While loneliness hurts, being connected to others feels good. We generally like being part of groups. It generally feels safe. Proof: SO many clubs, team sports, churches, college Greek systems, family reunions, fellowships, raves, cults, rallies, and on and on and on. That is all before we talk about the holy grail of connection: romantic partnerships. The dating apps, reality television shows, and the wedding industry depend upon this holy grail quest.

And...pets. We have so many pets. Whether they are officially designated for emotional support or not, that's what they do. They provide connection. So we clean up after them and buy them expensive food and outfits and call them our babies.

Recall from Chapter 1 that the teenage drive for peer connection is particularly strong. The prehistoric teenager did better in the wild world when rolling with a crew.

And yet parents are as critical as ever

While we know the cafeteria table of characters prioritizes bonding with each other over bonding with the likes of you, your connection to your kid is critical for two reasons:

One, family connections model what relationships with others look like. Good relationships at home provide your kid with a template of how a relationship should feel. Good relationships at home increase the odds your kid will fall in with a healthy, supportive crew. People gravitate toward relationships that feel similar to the ones watched and experienced while growing up. If you've ever been in therapy, I'm betting they made you talk about your childhood family relationships. Those relationships planted the seeds of how you engage with people as an adult.

Two—and this is the big one—*you are the backup crew. You are the safety net crew.*

Your kid may have trouble finding their people out there. Something could go wrong with a key friendship. Your kid may get dumped by their first love. The group your kid was once part of may start to suck and evolve away from your kid. Maybe your kid is just too cool for the rest of them. This is where the home is called into play. You are there to mitigate any loneliness Peer World may have dealt your kid. You want your kid to turn to you. You being stable and your kid knowing how important they are to you are prerequisites to Connection. Connection is the relationship.

You may assume that because y'all live in the same house, y'all feel connected to each other. Do not assume anything. Be deliberate in the care and feeding of your relationship with your kid.

If you would like an eye roll, tell your kid, "I would like to build a Connection with you." No, you, Dear Parent, are not that much of a dork. Rather, build Connection via side doors. Suggestions incoming.

Read what they read and watch what they watch

Read and watch what they are reading and watching. You don't have to want to. You don't have to like it. Do it to cultivate neutral topics of conversation. I could give two shits about the Seattle Seahawks, but when my son was away at school, I watched them because he watched them. It gave us another phone conversation topic.

Reality TV can be distasteful and moronic. However, for conversation topics, reality TV is a gold mine. Disturbing, funny, and ridiculous are par for the course. If you and your kid are watching the same show, you get to engage in the original connector activity: gossip. There is always something to talk about—the good, the bad, and the ugly.

Watch the shows they are watching that include complicated teenage characters. You may get to have a conversation about those characters. You may get an opportunity to talk about sex, drugs, school, and friendships. It will be more comfortable for both you and your darling to talk about these topics while talking about fictional characters. You may get opportunities to ask, "Is that really a thing?" "Do you know anyone like that?" "Are there people at your school like that?"

Loads of families have bonded over *Harry Potter*. You may have to read some books not nearly as universally well liked as Harry Potter. I think someone always dies in the John Green books, but teenagers seem to love them.

Reader beware: You may read the books and not be thrilled your kid is reading them. I binged on the *Twilight* books by Stephenie Meyer. A good story is a good story. And the movies were once all the rage. Now, whether one is Team Edward or Team Jacob (Team Edward, 100 percent), the story is disturbing—particularly the second book. Bella courts danger in order to hear the voice of the *VAMPIRE* boy who *left her*. Nope, it was not okay. However, whether you like it or not, your kids are reading and watching all sorts of troubling things. Give some thought to *The Little*

> "To some people, the original is their favorite thing in the world, the movie that made them love horror, that Mom or Dad showed them when they were ten that bonded them together."
>
> —SCREAM (1996)

Mermaid. It's pretty messed up. Read and watch just to be in the conversation, for better or worse.

Caveat: Don't sit them down for a book club or interrogate them about a movie. The goal here is to have random topics of conversation for when you are together, like in the car or at the dinner table.

Seek random topics you can just start talking about. If no one bites and engages, move along like you've just entertained yourself. Example: "Did you know that pandas being released into the wild need to have not been around people, so the caretakers dress up like pandas and spray panda pee on themselves?" Years from now your kids may recall, "Remember when Mom used to try to get us talking by bringing up shit about pandas?" Then you, Dear Parent, have crushed it. Your kids will know you were giving it an effort.

Do stuff together

Do whatever they want to do that they will do with you. I sat through the movie *V for Vendetta* twice because my son wanted to. I didn't like the movie the first time. Play the damn video games. They can't be worse than Chutes and Ladders.

Do not try to get your kid to do what you want to do. Figure out what they would want to do (or at least tolerate doing with you) and do that. Do any sort of shared activity you can afford. Even the most reluctant kid will do cool stuff with you when you pay. I propose that your best parenting money is spent on having fun with your kid.

Regularly eat together, without screens. Have a once-a-week pizza night or Chinese takeout or whatever. Have Sunday dinner or Saturday morning doughnuts or pancakes. If your family is too busy to regularly eat together, then your family is too busy.

Important paragraph ahead...

This is more important than one paragraph at the end of the chapter may imply. The activities suggested here are for the purposes of building Stability, Importance, and Connection. They are not rewards. They are not to be taken away as punishment. If you planned on a fun day of whatever for the sake of having fun with your kid, you don't take it away because they made an unfortunate choice and did something stupid, dangerous, or even illegal. If the kid is making stupid choices, all the more reason you need to spend time with them.

> *"Remember when it used to be, 'Daddy's home!'? Now, nothing. We watch TV in four separate rooms, and we IM each other when dinner's ready."*
>
> —RV (2006)

CHAPTER 7: DON'TS

Just Because You Have a Teenager in the House, You Don't Have to Be an Asshole About It

Jocko Willink, former Navy Seal and all-around cool dude, brought this chapter together. I wrote a bossy list for you, and Jocko provided the "why." In his MasterClass, Critical Leadership Training, Willink is clear that you cannot lead (read: influence) people without them trusting you. Influence—you want that! So...you are well advised to protect your kid's trust in you. It is really hard to repair broken trust; you know this. So double down on protecting your kid's trust in you. Without further ado...

Do not accuse deceit

Don't accuse your kid of lying, deceit, deception, duplicity, fraud, chicanery, or mendacity. Remove those words from your family vocabulary. What if they are obviously lying and totally insulting your intelligence? NO. EVEN when they are obviously LYING. When you know someone well and you pay attention, you can spot lying. Some people immediately go on the offensive when they are lying. Once you see it, it's sort of funny. Except, of course, when it isn't.

Don't call out obvious lying, because…the goal here is being *effective*, not "right." By effective, I mean protecting the relationship and thereby protecting your influence. When you call out dishonesty, you won't gain anything. Best case, you are right. So good for you; you win. You busted them and you're right. But you won't win a trophy, not even a stupid, half-assed participation trophy. Your "win" would mean someone lost, which is competition, not relationship.

There is also a serious risk to accusing them of lying. You could be wrong, which would be a hit to the relationship. From 1982, a true story—I lived it. I was sixteen. I had smoked pot a couple times with the Easy-to-Dislike boyfriend. My parents decided I had been regularly and recently smoking pot. However, they were wrong. When confronted, I answered truthfully. Yes, I had, but I didn't really like it and had not partaken in over a month.

Pause. This was the best-case scenario: I didn't want to smoke pot. The shithead was not turning me into the druggie of parental nightmares. He was just an asshole. This best-case scenario got blown to hell. My parents did not believe me. They said I "was telling stories." I was not.

If you wrongly accuse anyone, let alone your kid, of lying, you will look like (1) the enemy and (2) an asshole. You put your kid in a powerless scenario; it is difficult to prove a negative, such as "I am not lying." My conclusion at the time was "These people do not have my back." Consequence of this conclusion? They lost any credibility they may have had. I stopped going to them for guidance or support. While relationships with our parents are long and complicated and neither all good nor all bad, and my parents didn't know better, it was a grenade to the relationship.

There are ways to communicate skepticism. If you think what you are being told isn't totally on the up-and-up, say, "It really looks like _____." "I don't know that that makes sense to me." "I'm not sure what I think about that." Getting creative at ways to respond to them can distract you from your darling probably lying to your face and you wanting to hit them upside their fool head. You do not have to say you believe what they are saying. If they are lying, they will know they are lying, they aren't going to feel great about it, and they are going to be fairly sure you know they are lying—your kid is 100 percent not stupid. Everyone will know what's going on—without your accusation and their defense. That sort of power struggle strains relationships. Likewise…

Do not lie to them

Model honesty and authenticity. Honesty carries the responsibility of discernment. If they ask you a question (Parent Gold Star for you!), answer with facts. Any tales of debauchery or related glory can be saved for your class reunion. Answer with what happened and what you were thinking, or not thinking, at the time. If they are still listening, add what you now think about the situation. Be human.

I think the Drug-Free 'Merica people advise not telling your kids about your own drug or alcohol use so that you don't give them the ammunition to say, "But you did…" It is fine if your darling lobs this at you because by having an honest discourse about your own choices, you get opportunities to say, "This is why I wish I hadn't in that situation," or "This is what I worry about with you doing what I did." You have an opening to tell them what you've learned. This is a good thing, Drug-Free 'Merica people.

Trust is also about their ability to entrust, so...

Do not betray their confidence

When your kid tells you something (they are talking to you! Go You!) it is not for you to repeat. Your kid's confidences shared with you should be as sacrosanct as if you were their therapist. Which means there are exceptions: you are told someone poses an imminent danger to themselves or others, or you suspect child abuse. Your kid should know that you will hold things they share with you as private, but you will have to break that confidence if someone is in direct danger. Your kid should be able to trust you to not break confidence without first telling them.

Do not read their journal

IT IS NONE OF YOUR BUSINESS, and it is just wrong. Your kid, as much as everyone, has the right to their own thoughts and to decide with whom to share their thoughts and secrets. Do not take away their right to vent and bitch and be totally honest privately. Journaling can be a way to process confusion and sadness and despair. It is a way to sort out our mental messes. There isn't a filter requirement (one of the therapy benefits—we can be truly honest without judgment). It only works when it is truly private. Don't take that away from your kid. If you read their journal, you are saying that you would hook them up to a mind-reading machine were it available. How would you like to have that done to you, particularly if you are struggling?

Also problematic, you may read it wrong or out of context. My journal doesn't include backstory, context, explanation, or fact-checking. I have thought and journaled terrible, hateful things, in the moment, from painful places, unjustified and bitchy places. Your kid has the right to do this. My parents read my journal when they feared I was becoming a teen druggie. While fear motivated them, it was still betrayal. They doubled down on the betrayal by then using my journal as evidence against my honesty. (I hadn't bolded the past tense in MY JOURNAL in order to keep things clear for a reader.) Their poor choices have faded from relevancy over the forty-plus years since, and my parents were much more than a few ineffective choices during a stressful time. However, I still judge this betrayal as having been stupid and destructive.

I don't think you, Dear Parent, are lazy, and reading your kid's journal is lazy. If you are worried about the choices they are making, don't investigate in the shadows. If they are significantly late for curfew, start calling around, or get in the car and drive around. If you are worried that they are running with the wrong kids, or doing smack, or building bombs, scan their spaces. If you are afraid, level up your attention on their life. Spend more time with them. The greater your fear, the greater the time. Force a family road trip; drop other family activities into their laps. First, whatever time you hijack is less

> *"You read her diaries? Oh, that is gross! That's bad. 'Bad Mom' award."*
>
> —FREAKY FRIDAY (2003)

time available for any nonsense. Second, you are investing in your connection with them, which will be the ground from which you can encourage them away from dangerous and sketchy activities and people.

Pay attention to your kid, their life, and their moods. Pay attention to what they are doing with their money and time. If there's something that doesn't feel right, pay even more attention and spend even more time with them. Offer them a therapist as just someone for them to talk to who isn't you. Don't send them to a therapist as any sort of punishment or to fix them. If your kid doesn't like the first therapist, keep looking until you find one they do.

Relationships require trust. Even if, for some reason, you don't trust the little monster as far as you can throw them, you still need them to trust you. If your kid has stormed out and told you to go fuck yourself and they are joining the fucking carnival because it would be better than being in your fucking house looking at your hypocritical fucking life, the journal is still off limits. You won't need the journal to find them; they'll be at the highest-paying carnival.

If you've read their journal, do not do it again. If you haven't been caught, turn your mind away from anything you've read; it isn't admissible in court. Admit nothing—I don't know that there is a statute of limitations on this betrayal. If caught, apologize with absolutely everything you have.

Do not play the role of parole officer

Don't randomly track their location with their phone or another GPS. Generations of people grew up just fine without their parents knowing their every move. I like people being able to find each other, BUT don't use it unless you fear the kid is missing or stranded somewhere. If a kid is being treated like a parolee whose movements are monitored by their phone, they will just leave their phone wherever they are supposed to be. Duh. Your reward for your diligent parole officer parenting? A kid that is out God knows where doing God knows what without a phone. Which means they are out there without the ability to phone home. It would be great fun if their phones allowed us to see a location and then yell loudly at them through the phone, "Get the hell out of there!" Since that option does not exist as of this writing, leave the GPS alone.

Do not tell them "I'll be checking." Do not drug test. These actions are for parole officers. Sure, it is a scary world out there. The dangers and the risks are real. You are going to feel anxiety. People often attempt to allay fear and anxiety with control tactics. Authoritarian rules and demands. Surveillance. Tests and proof of compliance. Problem One: You don't have control over a human being whose job it is to grow away from you. You do have influence, if you have a relationship, which you will have if they trust you. Problem Two: Even if you sacrifice relationship building in order to control for their safety, you still cannot protect them from every awful thing that can happen in the world.

By prioritizing the connection you have with your kid, you are controlling what you can. By controlling yourself and your approach to the relationship with your kid, you are giving yourself the best chance of influencing their choices. This is the best way to prevent them from ending up with an actual parole officer.

Do not be a bad apologizer

When you screw up, my perfect human parent, apologize. And do it right. If the phrase "I am sorry you feel that way" is included, it is not an apology. The literal words do not include a recognition of your action. The other person won't feel apologized to. If you then say, "I said I was sorry," you look like an asshole. Do not pull this with your kid. An actual apology sounds like "I am *sorry for what I did* and that it made you feel that way." A good apology incites trust. It indicates that you aren't reckless in your relationship with them.

Don't cheapen the apology by justifying your actions. Your screw-up may have been honest, and your actions may have seemed justified to you. If asked why you did something, answer. If not asked, no one is interested in your why. HUMILITY IS YOUR FRIEND. An effective apology comes from a place of actual regret. Look at the person you are apologizing to. We can feel when we receive a heartfelt, honest apology.

If you are feeling defensive or resentful about needing to apologize, you aren't ready to apologize yet. Take time away from the situation, and validate your own feelings and humanity. Humans make mistakes. Being able to accept yourself as fallible will enable you to be a good apologizer.

A genuine apology is quite simple. "I am sorry I did/said/forgot ____. I am happy to hear whatever you want to say." Then patiently listen (if they're talking, that's a win). Patient, present listening is a powerful way to make amends.

I worked with a woman who had felt so betrayed by her parents that she had their severed heads tattooed on her arm. I don't think your kids will do that.

Do not freak out

It is unpleasant to be around someone who is freaking out or losing their shit. It can look like yelling, crying, maybe throwing something or slamming a cupboard, maybe making threats and condemnations and telling someone just exactly how much what they just said or did sucks. Someone losing their shit feels stressful to everyone present. The environment becomes less certain, more fraught.

Staying calm when someone else is having an emotional outburst helps that person calm down. Staying calm will serve you well when dealing with an emotions-running-high teenager. If another person is riled up and you stay calm, you won't add fuel to their fire. If you tell them to calm down, you will really piss them off. When you tell someone to calm down, they are hearing "I don't care about your feelings," which can translate to "I don't care about you." Being emotional is exhausting; people do calm down. And they calm down much more quickly when people around them stay calm and allow them to.

Staying calm fosters trust. When a person is calm, we trust them to hear us. We trust they are listening. We trust they are emotionally able to be there for us. If I tell you something controversial, or troubling, or frightening and then have to deal with your emotional overrun, I will stop talking. I will also think twice before coming to you again with a difficult topic because I won't trust you to hear me.

In his freshman year of high school, my son went through a rough patch. He was at a private boarding school and wanted to leave. We sat in a diner booth late at night as he told me how unhappy he was. It scared me, and my tears were right there. Over and over in my head played, "Don't freak out. You can freak out later, away from him. You can cry as much as you want, but not now." Over and over I silently played this chorus to myself. What I said, and to this day think was one of my better parenting moments, was "I don't know what the right choice is. But I will stay here until it's figured out. Never make a big decision on a bad day." Twenty-four hours later he decided for himself to stay at the school, and four years later graduated from there with stories and accomplishments and his future groomsmen.

Ask questions with humility and curiosity. If you ask a question and your kid answers honestly, don't ruin the moment by freaking out and jumping all over them because you don't like their answer. Stay calm. Do not make them regret speaking with you.

Freaking out is the enemy of all that is holy. If you are feeling your face getting warm, your blood pressure rising, whatever it is for you, take a break. You are emotionally flooding. Your lizard brain has been activated, and your own prefrontal cortex functioning will be impaired. Separate yourself from the situation. Go ahead and lose your mind, regroup, and then return. You don't have to know what to do. You can say, "I am angry. I am scared of this. I don't know what to do. I need to think about this." Spend ten to fifteen minutes away to just breathe and calm down. The very worst part of flooding is that we don't lose our ability to speak. The odds of saying destructive and ineffective things will be high. All of the worst things I've said to other people have been when I was emotionally flooded. All of the worst things said to me have come from someone who was emotionally flooded. Having conversations with a teen human, particularly in a fraught situation, is the big leagues. You need to be at your best. Do what you need to be calm. I am not averse to a bit of Xanax.

Let's say your kid has been arrested for drunk driving.

Clearly this is not okay. Everything about it is terrifying. Losing your shit would be expected. I'd want to shake the kid and yell, "HOW COULD YOU DO THIS?" And maybe I would because it is just TOO MUCH. The reaction would be appropriate. However, it wouldn't be helpful. Keep your eye on the prize, people. And don't try dealing with a drunk.

Here is the problem with losing your shit in such a situation. When your emotions are high—and this scenario would send my emotions off the chart—it is not the time to problem-solve or communicate all the better choices the goddamn kid could have made. The goal is not to be righteous and show them what a goddamn idiot they have been, because it won't make it better. The overarching goal is to protect the relationship. Your power to influence your kid lies within the quality of your relationship. And this drunken idiot will need your influence.

If you are like most of us and not a Dalai Lama spiritual master, you may have lost your shit. Do whatever you have to do to calm down. There is a lot of guidance out there, and everyone is different. You probably know what calms you down. YouTube and podcasts will give you a kazillion techniques. Find something that works. Cry until you are too exhausted to freak out. Find a Navy Seal breathing exercise.

After you've calmed down, and when everyone is sober, comes the apology. "I'm sorry I lost my shit."

Next, "I'm not at all thrilled about the circumstances, but I am relieved to see you. This terrified me. And I hate to be terrified. This is bad, really bad. But I am here, and I've got your back, and I am here to help *YOU* work through figuring out *YOUR* next steps for this shit show."

Next, ask calmly and with genuine interest, "How the fuck did this happen?" Then listen.

Do not be an adversary

Your love is supposed to be unconditional. So act like it is. No, you don't buy balloons and hire a clown if they have just gotten arrested. (Plus, clowns suck.) Your being there for your kid isn't something they have to earn; therefore, it isn't something they should be able to lose.

Being glad, including relieved, to see them is not the same as being happy with whatever they've done or said. The most law-abiding among the teenage darlings will probably imitate an idiot sometimes. (Seventeen-year-old me regularly rode with an actual Eagle Scout who liked to turn the headlights off while driving country roads at night.)

You can, and should, be crystal clear about not liking a choice your teenage darling made. The action is not the kid. You do not need to condone an action or look away from choices that you don't like or that scare you. You do not have to solve their problems. (Rarely should you, actually.) You can be livid about the absolute dipshit choice they made. At the same time, do not withhold love and kindness from your kid.

A more moderate example: Let's say your darling comes home after curfew. You were worried, this scared you, you couldn't sleep, it was inconsiderate and irresponsible, and you are so pissed and would like to hit them over their fool head. However, access what is most true: "I'm glad you are home. Are you all right?" "I want to talk in the morning. Let me know if you need anything." You do not know what has gone on out there in Peer World. Maybe shenanigans, pranks, or foolishness. Maybe dangerous things have gone on. Maybe they have gotten their heart broken.

When in doubt, just be happy to see them.

You, Dear Parent, are also human. Somewhere along the

way, a day may come when you are absolutely not okay with something that has gone on and you don't know what to do. Say, "I have no idea what to do." "I don't know how to be useful right now." "I need to think." Then reach out for support.

You can also shake your head and say to yourself, "Fuck me. They are owning the shit out of being sixteen."

> "If we don't start trusting our children, how will they ever become trustworthy?"
>
> —*FOOTLOOSE* (1984)

PART THREE

The Minefields

Minefields are places where things can quickly go terribly wrong: School. Peers. Sex. Drugs. This is the stuff that keeps parents up at night. Parts 1 and 2 provided the groundwork, all for the purpose of building a relationship from which to parent (influence) your kid as they navigate teenage minefields.

I want your kid to be happy and secure and have great relationships with you and other adults and peers. I want them to be excited about life and able to experience real fun and joy and connection without being impaired.

Physical danger doesn't typically reside within the arenas of school and peers, but angst and drama do. If you navigate these well, you set up your relationship to better navigate the minefields of sex and drugs, where the angst and drama not only tend to be more intense, but are also accompanied by physical, emotional, and legal danger.

Here's the thing about a minefield: You can't drag someone out. However, you are not powerless. Your power is your ability to encourage and guide them to safely navigate their own way out of a minefield.

CHAPTER 8: SCHOOL

But Will It Be on the Test?

So much attention and controversy and discord around school and grades get played out between parents and their offspring—attention and drama that may be misplaced.

Grades—oh, how parents talk about grades. We have these hopes and dreams for our kids. Grades determine those immediate post–high school options. Bad grades can eliminate a lot of those options. We wring our hands and fret about the bad grades and ask, "Doesn't the damn kid understand the consequences? (I've been there, done that; it didn't help.) They won't get into the school they (or is it we?) want." I propose that vigilant grade watching and homework tracking are not great uses of your limited energy and influence. We're playing the long game, and your kid's high school performance does not determine how their long game will play out.

Grades have consequences, yes. However, not the really bad consequences like permanent injury, jail, overdose, pregnancy, and STDs. Those are the actual dangers. Bad grades aren't any of those things. I'm not defining Good Grades versus Bad Grades. Good means whatever good means to you, and Bad means whatever bad means to you. Good grades evidence a couple good things. But are they overarching obsession worthy?

Good Thing One. Good grades provide opportunities for scholarships and college choices. Good grades tell the world that the kid not only has a reasonable level of intelligence, but also works hard. Knowledge is power, knowing stuff is cool, and accomplishments feel good. All true, and I want good grades for your kid as much as you do. These are undeniable benefits of good grades. However, if the scholarship and college choices aren't what you'd like them to be, how bad is that really? Now more than ever before, there are opportunities to learn and develop oneself without heading to Harvard at eighteen. If the dream school says, "No thank you," your kid is not sentenced to a crappy, financially insecure life.

When your darling decides to care about learning, they will find a path. Outside of traditional high school, there are online courses, GED courses, community colleges, and trade schools, all of which can be done part-time while your kid is working and earning their way. Each of these avenues provides opportunities to demonstrate ambition and mastery and can be leveraged into higher levels of education or professional development. For whatever reason, some people are late academic bloomers. Maybe academics aren't

> *"Well, some teachers were trying to low-ball me, Daddy. And I know how you say, 'Never accept a first offer,' so I figure these grades are just a jumping-off point to start negotiations."*
>
> —CLUELESS (1995)

ever their thing and they build a great life with a trade or entrepreneurship.

Even if your fabulous eighteen-year-old heads off to Super Dream School and you have the bumper sticker and sweatshirt to prove it, they will still have to make their way through that school and into the professional world. That acceptance letter on beautiful letterhead does not set them up for life; it is just a nice starting block. Kids can also get into that great, dreamy college, crash and burn, and then later get back onto an academic track, or not. An affluent local family was very attached to their son going to Pepperdine. He wanted to take a year off of school. So he did both and had a fun year, without learning much, on the stunning (and expensive) Pepperdine campus.

A short-term lack of educational opportunities is not a life sentence from which your kid can never take charge of their life and get educated and/or grow financially and professionally. Bad grades are not, in reality, dangerous.

If you have a kid who wants to go to a competitive college and wants to do the work to get in—the activities, AP classes, test prep courses, and so on—excellent! Encourage and support them, of course. Just because this is a great thing doesn't mean it is terrible if your kid could currently give two shits about school.

Good Thing Two. In addition to good grades (and test scores and prestigious college acceptance letters) providing opportunities, they also evidence a capable, headed-for-greatness kid, which reflects well on you, the brilliant parent.

You like the reflection of your kid's accomplishments on you. We just do; it's all right to admit it. Parents brag about their kids' accomplishments all the time. I've listened to the following more than once. Parent A: "Chucky has done SO COOL THIS and won CAN YOU BELIEVE IT THAT." Parent B: "Pennywise did AMAZING THAT, and then got asked to perform CAN YOU BELIEVE IT THAT." And then Parent C joins in about their kid, Candyman, and so on. These conversations include an undercurrent of parental self-congratulation and unspoken proclamation of "See how great a parent I am, obviously, and how great our gene pool is. We're so lucky to be so smart."

Of course we are proud of our kids and want to tell people. Even grandparents get in on the game. I heard this endearing brag by a woman proudly referring to her granddaughter: "She's almost above average!"

While we support our kids' accomplishments, the accomplishments aren't ours. When we blur the lines between what is ours to do and what is our kids' to do, it can get dark. Think 2019 college admissions scandal, often referred to as "Operation Varsity Blues." Rick Singer, as the mastermind/center of the travesty, collected millions of dollars to get kids into elite colleges via cheating and fraud. He's quoted as saying, "Saturday night—it is an amazing night. Why? Because Mom and Dad go to a dinner party. They hear about every kid who's getting into this school, going to this summer program, doing this, doing that. Sunday morning, my phone rings off the hook."[10]

For a deep dive into this demonstration of entitlement and greed, listen to Season 1 of the podcast *Gangster Capitalism*. If a kid hadn't done the work to get the desired test score, the parent could pay Singer to get the test taken by someone else.

---

[10] Rick Singer, "College Bribery Ringleader Auditioned for Reality Show on College Admissions... Here's How You Play the Game," video, TMZ, March 13, 2019, https://www.tmz.com/2019/03/13/william-rick-singer-ringleader-reality-show-audition-college-bribery/.

The parents often then decided to hide this purchase and let the kid think they'd earned the good score. For irony: Jane Buckingham, with her husband, cowrote a story for *Time* magazine about the problems with being helicopter parents, hovering over their kid's every move. She did parent speaking engagements. She also pleaded guilty to paying Singer $50,000 to arrange a proctor to take the ACT for her kid. That's awkward, Jane.

There's a flip side to feeling you deserve some credit for your kid's accomplishments. It is feeling shame when YOUR kid isn't on track toward AMAZING-CAN-YOU-BELIEVE-IT classic accomplishments.

Parents easily mistake their kid as their possession, their trophy, or their parental report card. Your kid is not your possession, your trophy, or your report card.

Let's say your kid is scraping by in a class (or classes), or straight up failing, and the kid does not appear to care. Then you run into Parent A, from above, who shares that Chucky got a full-ride scholarship to the Institute of Amazing, earned with their grades at their Super Smart School. This isn't going to feel good to you. You feel something like envy, but not really. You love your kid; you don't want to trade. Chucky is a weird kid anyway. But Shame could knock at your door. Don't let that bastard in. Shame will never help you. Augusten Burroughs, author of bestselling memoir *Running with Scissors*, calls shame a landfill emotion. It comes from the accepting of other people's garbage about how things "should" be.

School is just a life season

Life is a long game, no one makes it out alive, and most people will have struggles and failures and get hit with shit storms of their own making and shit storms not of their own making. If your kid is currently sucking at school, you hold your head high, express no shame, and double down on Part 2 of this book. Build ground from which to listen, support, guide, and influence. In other words, parent.

CODE ORANGE ALERT: Pay attention to grades not as the necessary ingredients for a good FUTURE life, but as signposts of the health of your kid's *CURRENT* life. Bad grades can be a Code Orange alert of other problems and a signal to you to look even more closely at your kid's life than you already have been. *THIS is the usefulness of grades.* Grades don't happen in a vacuum. They aren't random. If your kid's grades suck, figure out why.

Maybe your kid is just all about the social and being with friends. Studying something with no immediate application to their lives isn't competing well against being with friends. This kid could be the future sales professional outearning the valedictorian. Chapter 1's cafeteria table of characters may be way more interesting than algebra. No Code Orange escalation necessary.

Or maybe your kid is all in on a particular sport or some other time-consuming activity, such as dance or drama. Of their remaining available time, socializing and sleeping may take precedence over studying. No Code Orange escalation necessary.

Or...there's a problem. Maybe a learning challenge has shown up. Your teenager could be in the middle of relationship drama, heartbreak, or mistreatment by a friend or romantic interest, and they don't have the mental or emotional bandwidth for learning history. Maybe they are smoking pot, and their memory function is not what it should be.

Have the grades conversations

Once you've figured out what's going on with the grades and you decide how you want to address whatever is going on with your kid, THEN bring up the topic of grades. By this point you will have established with your kid that their well-being is more important to you than their grades. This is what they most want to know.

Watch for a moment when you can ask "What's going on with the grades?" NOT "Hey, Dumbass, why do these grades suck so bad?" You are asking not as a prosecutor interrogating a defendant, but as a curious person interested in the answer. If you sense your kid is shutting down and not really listening or talking, let it go for now. Watch for your next opening and start the conversation again. When your darling seems to be listening, tell them why the grades worry you. If you aren't sure specifically what to say, fall back on "I'm the parent, and this worry is part of my job description."

Ask whether the grades bother them. Ask them whether they want any sort of assistance in improving them. Until your darling actually wants better grades, there isn't a lot you can do. Be supportive of *their* efforts. Help *them* organize studying. Help *them* put boundaries around other activities to allow for focused study. Do not make the grades a "we" problem.

Unless…there is some sort of learning disability or other learning challenge that your kid has been able to compensate for up until now. Then, you, Dear Parent, need to get the appropriate support to help them.

If your kid is struggling in a subject and they don't want to be, work with them. Get a friend who knows the topic to work with them. If you can, hire a tutor. But the work and the grades are on your kid. Keep the results in their lane. Do not take away work. Do not sit there and do homework with them. Don't be that parent who says, "we got homework done." I suspect you passed ninth grade. You do not need to do the homework again.

If your darling wants to do better in school and you have some credibility with them (Go You!) look for people on YouTube teaching study habits. Your kid may be more interested in what an "expert" thinks over the likes of you.

School is not a "we" project

After age eleven, refrain from telling a teacher what your kid should or should not have to do. Do not argue about grades with teachers. Let your kid (1) deal with failure and decide whether to work harder, (2) adapt to a teacher or rules they don't like, and (3) ask a teacher for help. Most teachers would be so taken aback by a kid asking for help that they would probably fall over themselves to be helpful.

Your job when your kid is challenged by something that is disappointing, unfair, or general nonsense is to help them deal with it, not go in and eliminate any problems. There are mean, stupid, terrible bosses and jobs and neighbors and any number of other unpleasant and difficult people and circumstances out there waiting for them in the real world. Your kid starts learning in school how to deal with situations that aren't perfect. Kids need to learn to deal with teachers, coaches, umpires, and directors. Life will not always be fair.

Before you get your panties in a bunch, I did not say to

have your kid deal on their own with abusive or dangerous situations or anything involving a motel. Just know that a teacher who gives a bad grade or says something insensitive is not abusive or dangerous. A coach who yells at them is not abusive or dangerous. Your kid is not a fragile snowflake. Besides, the predatory teachers and coaches are going to be nice; they want to be liked—they aren't going to want to draw negative attention to themselves by being obvious assholes. A girl at a local private high school fell prey to a teacher's sexual advances. He was the *BELLS TEACHER*, which is not the first place you'd expect a predator. Then there's the supercreep USA Gymnastics doctor who got away with being a terrible human being for years because he seemed so nice. If you suspect a crime is being committed, or being set up to be committed, go in there and raise all holy hell.

Don't buy the carrots, and set down the sticks

I see parents attempt the carrot or stick strategies to get their kids to do better at school, but I don't know that I've ever seen them be effective. So I would say to you over coffee, keep the carrots and sticks out of it.

A popular carrot is paying for grades. I'm not a fan. The goal is to learn something. A grade is recognition of the learning. Being paid to do something can make a person value the work less and be less inclined to take an interest in it. You

> "Oh, I love seeing teachers outside of school. It's like seeing a dog walking on its hind legs."
>
> —MEAN GIRLS (2004)

don't need to take my word for it. Richard Ryan, PhD, and Edward Deci, PhD, developed the Self-Determination Theory (SDT) of motivation. These two performed loads of studies over the years showing that people are more motivated at challenging tasks by an internal reward, such as pride, than an external reward of money or prizes. For a deep dive, read the American Psychological Association article "The Intrinsic Motivation of Richard Ryan and Edward Deci." It states that "People certainly can be motivated externally—by money... but Deci and Ryan say that type of controlled motivation can actually taint a person's feelings about the basic worth of the project and undermine intrinsic motivation."[11] There have been studies where participants were paid or not paid to solve difficult puzzles or math problems. The paid participants gave up sooner. The unpaid participants stuck with challenges longer, presumably because they had an intrinsic motivation toward the satisfaction that comes from mastering a challenge.

Celebrate your kid's efforts, not the grade or trophy. Being able to be proud of effort independent of results will be more valuable in the game of life than a high school grade or trophy.

The sticks, I'm not a fan of those either. Don't ground, harp, nag, or rant about grades. I have never seen a demonstration that those things are effective in making someone say, "Oh, thanks, I never thought of it that way. Thank you for ranting. I'm ready to go read now."

---

[11] Delia O'Hara, "The Intrinsic Motivation of Richard Ryan and Edward Deci," American Psychological Association, 2017, https://www.apa.org/members/content/intrinsic-motivation.

What if they won't attend school?

If your kid is regularly skipping school, rather than taking an occasional Ferris Bueller day off, you need to figure out what the hell they are doing with their time and why they don't want to go to school. You double down on Stability/Importance/Connection and have the fraught conversations. Regular school skipping is a Code Orange alert for you to pay attention to what the hell is going on with your kid. It could be bad relationships, being bullied, being a social outcast, depression, severe anxiety, or something else. If drugs are involved, I submit to the court that something else is going on and making regular drug use a more attractive option than being at school with friends.

What if your little genius wants to drop out? First investigate, consistent with above. What the hell is going on? Maybe an alternative high school or online study program would be a good alternative. If you understand the underlying dropping-out motivation and you've done what you can to support your kid through whatever the underlying problem is and they still refuse to go to school, then they must be ready to get a job and support themselves. Some minimum wage work may quickly make school look pretty good to them.

CHAPTER 9: PEERS

Shakespearean Dramas and Greek Tragedies

Teenagers have been building crews of peers with whom to head into the unknown for eons. This process of leaving you behind has begun. And while you've known all along that they would grow away from you and toward new relationships, you wouldn't be the first parent to say, "Already?"

There will eventually be people who know your kid better than you do. Bittersweet, absolutely. Before you say No Way Jose, consider whether there is someone who knows you better than your parents do. As a mother I want to quietly say to my kids, "But I love you most. I loved you first." At the same time, I am grateful for the people who have come along and loved my kids. What more can you want for someone you love than for them to be loved? We want our kids to have intimate friends and partners who know and understand them. God willing, your kid will outlive you. You want them to have their own people. You want them to have someone with whom to bitch about you.

After meeting my first perfect newly born granddaughter, it was an ugly cry evening. There was so much emotion. I felt overwhelming relief that this giant ten-pound baby was healthy and this was therefore one more time I could know that my son was all right. There was full-on gratitude in those tears. And also, it hurt to not be part of this giant baby's inner family pod with my son and daughter-in-law. I was now someone's extended family. I would have happily held that giant baby for the next year.

The joy of your darling growing up and building their own crews and families is SO GOOD. Also, being left behind stings a bit. You don't have to like it.

The first Christmas that my son came home from school out-of-state, I was an inner mess. I couldn't enjoy the time. What I clearly remember about those three weeks is thinking about little else other than "He's leaving again. He's not staying here. He's leaving again," over and over. I was bracing for the grief that was lying in wait for me when the break ended.

Raise the curtains, the drama has begun

Recall the cafeteria table cast of characters surrounded by other cafeteria tables of like characters, all of them important to each other. Recall Dopamine with the entourage of EasilyBored, ThrillSeeker, and Impulsive. HighEmotions and Amorous are there too. PreFrontalCortex is around somewhere, but hard to find. Of course there is drama. There are cliques and friendships and childhood friends taking different paths and alliances forming and breaking and who's in and who's not. And where Amorous is, confusion and heartbreak are on the table.

There's a common adult imagining of how fun it would be to go back to high school knowing what they know now.

But going back knowing as little as the teenager they once were, no way in hell. The place was unforgiving.

Being secure in ourselves and our choices and our relationships takes some of us decades to learn. The self-help industry would crash if it didn't. Teenagers are trying to figure it all out amongst a bunch of other teenagers on the unforgiving stage of high school. Oh, and now everything gets filmed. It's all more than a bit fraught.

As noted earlier, you are the backup crew. You build and protect your relationship with your darling so that you can be there for them when shit gets real. Maybe they'll talk to you, and maybe you'll get to offer some wisdom. I'm not promising they'll think you have any idea what you are talking about, but maybe.

That half-assed PreFrontalCortex is a factor in more than just good decision-making. Our adult prefrontal cortexes are the source of our knowledge that circumstances and feelings change, that there is always a bigger picture, that whatever hell is happening, it won't be forever. Your darling hasn't yet gotten to see the other side of any first-time drama/pain/bullshit they may be dealing with. Without PreFrontalCortex fully in the game, they won't necessarily know there is another side.

There's a reason they don't just go from being your agreeable child who wants to do everything with you one day to heading off into the world with their forever friends and partners the next day. Relationships require skill and discernment, and these few teenage years are their chance to practice

> "She's my best friend. God, I hate her."
>
> —*HEATHERS* (1988)

while you are waiting at home for them. Home should be that steady spot where they can find a parent to whom they are important and connected to, no matter what is going on out there in Peer World.

It totally might look like a cult

Even when the friendships are drama-free, they can appear a bit cultish. No, not like real cults with charismatic leaders grooming sex slaves and free labor. Teenagers can just look a bit cultish. They dress alike. They talk alike. They do alike. They clique up and provide social behavior expectations of one another.

You've been watching, and probably judging, your kid's friends all along. Who isn't polite? Who seems maybe a bit stupid? Who is a narcissist in training? In the toddler room, who was the biter? (One of my granddaughters took that job for a while. Someone had to do it.)

You are going to naturally judge the kids you like and the kids you don't like because we do that. I've never really been a kid person. I adore mine. I adore my kid's kids. Others, I like sometimes. Most I can take or leave, and a few I've adored and would happily adopt. A few I've actively disliked. However, you don't get to curate your darling's friends. Don't sit up there in the cheap seats and decide that some of your kid's friends are a bad influence. They might be, but that's not the point. Your kid chose to hang with them for a reason. That reason is what you want to figure out. Your kid might be the bad influence. I worked with a high school classmate's mother. She would say about him, "He's a good boy, but his friends are such a bad influence." Her kid was the bad influence everyone else should have stayed away from.

If you think there is a high ratio of ding-dongs or kids who seem particularly parent-avoidant hanging around, your mission is to figure out the attraction your kid has to that group. You may not like an individual friend for any number of reasons. However, you don't know everything. Maybe that is the friend who's been there for your kid on rough days. Maybe that is the friend who makes your kid laugh when a laugh is needed.

You may be tempted to insert yourself into their Peer World by being their friend. Your relationship as your darling's parent is way more important and sacred than that of friend. You are the constant and the guide. Friendships evolve and change and fade. Your responsibility to parent is unconditional and unwavering. Referring to struggling kids, a high school teacher told me, "They really just want parents."

Listening is your superpower

Remember, *please*, the goal is not to tell them what to think and what to do. Agenda Item One: Let your darling feel heard, seen, important, loved, accepted, and sane. Just drop whatever you are doing and first listen. Pull out your old Stephen Covey "Seek first to understand"[12]—which can be difficult. You could go back to high school knowing what you know now and *RULE* the place. That is true because what you know now you learned for yourself, on the job of high school.

Agenda Item Two: Consider whether you understand how they are feeling and thinking. Understanding does not require agreement. If you have a question to ask, don't do so like you are opposing counsel. Access curiosity. Be respectful, *EVEN*

---

[12] Steven Covey, *The Seven Habits of Highly Effective People* (Free Press, 2004), 237.

if you want to say, "This is absolute batshit." Say this with your inside-your-head voice.

THEN move forward with telling your darling what *you* think.

When your darling was younger, you were able to lay down rules and directives: "Say please and thank you." "Don't touch the fire." "Go to bed." It can be easy to forget you are now dealing with a teen human who is not nearly as malleable and responsive to direction as an eight-year-old. They are about as malleable and responsive to direction as three-year-olds.

If you want to be heard and considered, make sure you aren't communicating that what *you* think is what *they* should think. This differentiation is key to the communication kingdom.

When you do speak, here are some phrases for your consideration:

"I don't see it exactly that way, but I see how someone could."

"I'm your parent, so of course I'm not going to love that idea/choice/person, but I love you."

"I don't want you to do that because…"

"I'm worried about that relationship because…"

"I don't like them doing…"

"I'm afraid of this situation because…"

"I don't like that kid because…"

"I know it feels/looks that way, but from the cheap seats it looks kind of like…"

"When someone is pushing you to do something, consider what's in it for them and why they care whether or not you do it."

"Nothing good happens after midnight."

If they ask you a direct question, answer it honestly. Use your answers as opportunities to talk about what you remember, learned, or may have regretted.

Be very clear with your words. The above statements don't include "You shouldn't _____ because…" Your kid has the right to their own opinion. People do not like to be "should-ed" on. (I know, that's this whole book, but I just really wanted to tell you this stuff really badly.)

If you yourself are going through some drama, you don't want to be "should-ed" on. You want someone to care for you by listening to you. You want to feel not alone. You don't want others telling you how to feel. Maybe it's just me, but people telling me how to feel quickly pisses me off.

If your darling is upset and you don't know what to do or say, imagine what you would want from someone and do that. If your kid isn't talking about whatever is going on, don't try to force it. Just be around. Ask if you can get them anything. Just be around and be quiet.

If your kid wants it, and it isn't for punishment or to "fix" them, find a therapist who works with teenagers. Do not force this, and if the kid doesn't like one, find another one.

And they call it "Puppy Love"?

"Puppy Love" my ass. Puppies are the best; we love puppies. They are so sweet, even when they bite you with their puppy teeth and chew on the table. Young love? It may look sweet from the outside, and Puppy Love is such a Hallmark Card phrase. Who doesn't remember how hard it could be to navigate teenage relationships? How confusing? How easy it was to feel insecure, and afraid, and inadequate? The drama.

This quote, from teenage Bella in the movie *Twilight*, is perfectly what a teenager might say: "About three things I was absolutely positive. First, Edward was a vampire. Second, there was a part of him—and I didn't know how dominant that part might be—that thirsted for my blood. And third, I was unconditionally and irrevocably in love with him." So dramatic and unconcerned with potential downside.

Unrequited crushes? Ugh. Romantic breakups? Ugh. To the participants, who generally have no idea what they are doing, along with the upside come anxiety and uncertainty and heartbreak potential. Doberman Love is a better descriptor. It hurts when your kid hurts. It is nature's way of making sure we protect them. You may want to find the offending party and smack them upside the head. (Please don't.)

One little son of a bitch called my daughter crazy. I proposed, "If he thinks the Apple is crazy, perhaps he should meet the Tree."

> "That's why they call them crushes. If they were easy, they'd call 'em something else."
>
> —*SIXTEEN CANDLES* (1984)

CHAPTER 10: SEX

Amorous Walked into a Party

Sex is such an adult act. So ultimately intimate. So fraught with dangerous and emotionally painful potential. And that's before that terrorist, alcohol, arrives at the scene. More on that terrorist later.

Along with a smoking area at high school, slut-shaming was fully in play in the early eighties. The double standard was alive and well. Sex is plenty complicated without a double standard in play.

This chapter tilts more toward considering teenage girls than it does boys. Gender issues aside, fairly or unfairly, people tend to worry more about the girls. Even sans the double standard, their world feels more dangerous. Her body is the one that can get pregnant. Her emotions are more tied to sex than a teenage boy's tend to be.

> "The rumors of my promiscuity have been greatly exaggerated."
> —EASY A (2010)

I abhor the whole Purity Ring thing. The concept of a young girl promising her chastity to her father, who then gives it to her husband, is creepy. My kids know that to prevent me from going on an already-heard tangent, they should not mention Purity Rings (so wrong), Columbus (what an asshole), or *Avatar* (not that good).

Whomever your darling is attracted to, or whichever gender they identify as, be judgment-free about it. The issues specific to LGBTQ teenagers are better served by other people's books. What I most want is for no one to be shamed for their gender and sexuality identifications. I want everyone to respect and honor themselves by treating their bodies and their affections as their own to share only as they choose to, LGBTQ or not. Anything will be easier if you start here: Love your kid. Provide a stable home. Pay attention to them. Be connected to them.

The girls may not be getting slut-shamed, but are things actually better for them?

The kids these days would say I'm showing my age when I cringe at sexting, intimate photos, expected blow jobs, and sex being treated as no big deal. This seems like a new tyranny of expectations. Something about any of this being associated with equality and freedom feels like maybe the teenage girls have been played. Who's benefiting the most from all this? The rates of depression and unhappiness among teenage girls don't indicate that girls have gotten a much better deal than the prior generations of us who were slut-shamed.

In the quest to be liberated and not answer to the patriarchy, a lot of girls wear less and less and are less selective about their sexual partners. In the documentary *Miss Representa-*

tion (worth watching), a woman played the Meat Loaf song "Paradise by the Dashboard Light" for a group of teenage girls. In the song, the couple is parking, the boy is aiming to go all the way, and the girl demands that he promise to love her to the end of time. The listening teenage girls didn't get it. The song didn't make sense to them. The woman explained to them that in the olden days, the boys used to have to at least pretend to like us before we had sex with them.

I am nostalgic for a time before sexting. In *Behind Their Screens, What Teens Are Facing (and Adults Are Missing)*, Emily Weinstein and Carrie James address the nuances of sexting: "Sexting can be consensual and wanted by both parties. Sexts can be pressured or even actively coerced; the result of one person feeling uncertain about how else to navigate requests or even trapped by threats or blackmail. Sexts can also be shared without permission, as in the case of pictures that are sent to one person and then shared further without consent from the person who is featured."[13]

Of course we want to tell the kids "Don't sext," along with "Don't drink. Don't smoke. Don't do drugs. Don't have sex." But we know it isn't that simple. We know peer approval and relationships are paramount. We know long-term consequences don't get as much teenage consideration as we would like.

How the hell do I parent through this?

Your trying to stop this train is unlikely to make a difference. You know how I hate a control grab. The forces of growing

---

[13] Emily Weinstein and Carrie James, *Behind Their Screens: What Teens Are Facing (and Adults Are Missing)* (MIT Press, 2022), 95.

up and sexual maturity are great and powerful, more powerful than you. I know a fellow who, in high school, was caught in a compromising position with his girlfriend when her father came home earlier than expected. Thereafter, the fellow was forbidden to be in the house when no parents were home. So, routinely over the next year, he and the girlfriend had sex in the driveway.

Assume that your kid is engaging in conversations and activities you are uncomfortable with, and assume these are happening sooner than you think they are. The cafeteria of characters is thinking a lot about sex.

I was with a group of parents speaking with a school administrator outside our kids' high school dance. One of the parents asked, "What about grinding?" and I thought, "Oh my God, no, don't say that word, stop, I don't want to be part of this conversation, make it stop." The administrator deadpan answered, "We don't allow it." The inside-my-head voice said, "I don't want to be in a conversation about that word, and whatever this guy does or does not allow, I'm betting it's going on right now and the dance just started."

Worse than these hormonal teen humans running around as the blind leading the blind, they have easy access to free porn, much of which doesn't model healthy, respectful sex.

> "Whether or not you face the future, it happens, right?"
>
> —PRETTY IN PINK (1986)

Be part of the conversation

Every "should" I have preached to you in this book is intended to enable you to be in the fraught conversations with your darling; I want your voice to be included with all the other peer and real-world influences being lobbed at them.

Keep up any conversations you can about sex, consent, porn, and sexting. As with all conversations about fraught topics, ask questions without an agenda, and then listen and make sure you understand the answers. Appreciate the world your kid is in and how long-term consequences won't be at the forefront of their minds, but their peer relationships will be. If they believe you understand their reality, then (and then only maybe) will they deem you potentially credible.

Express no judgment about any sexual behavior you hear about. Watch the television shows *Euphoria* and *Skins* (UK version) as well as raunchy teenage comedies and party movies. Desensitize yourself to what seems terrifying and awful to you, knowing that it probably doesn't seem that way to your kid. I recently rewatched *Fast Times at Ridgemont High*. Although I see the talent of a young Sean Penn, the movie's sex and consequences are sad to adult me. Nothing about the movie was sad to teenage me.

Show no fear. (This is critical when dealing with toddlers, teenagers, and strange dogs.) Also, no judgment. Abhor shame. Remove the word "promiscuous" from your vocabulary. These rules are for discussing their lives, but also for anytime sex is being discussed in relation to anyone. For them to come to you if shit gets real, they need to not fear your judgment. They need to not be afraid of you being disappointed in them.

Enlist trustworthy nonparent adults

When your kid likes and trusts another nonparent adult, that adult may get to talk to your kid about sex. It is more comfortable to talk to nonparents about sex. No one really wants to talk about sex with their parents.

One of the cooler youth group things I've seen was a conversation among same-sex teenagers and adults. None of the adults were parents to any of the teenagers present. The teenagers wrote questions anonymously on pieces of paper, which were then drawn from the hat by the adults, who would then answer the question. It was random, and everyone was hearing the answer, so if another adult wanted to add something or express a different viewpoint, they could. No kid would feel self-conscious about the question they asked.

Beware of that terrorist, alcohol

I submit to the court that much of the time when sexual assault, manipulation, or a doesn't-feel-right choice occurs, that terrorist, alcohol, is involved. Alcohol reduces inhibitions (which are generally protective) and judgment (also generally protective). By making sure your kid understands how alcohol works, you are not condoning drinking. You are accepting that opportunities to partake will come along and you'd like your kid to be the least stupid possible.

Sexual behavior has been sold to girls as cool and a way they can be equal to boys, and drinking has gotten the same false advertising. Girls get enticed into showing how cool and equal to the boys they are by keeping up with them at drinking. Alcohol is processed differently by male and female bodies, even after adjusting for weight. Drink for drink, the girl is going to become more drunk. It's science and has nothing to do with gender politics.

A drunk person can't consent. People should be able to get as inebriated as they want and go wherever they want and still be safe from sexual assault. Absolutely. But that isn't how it always works. While slut-shaming may have existed in the eighties, we were free from thinking it within the realm of possibility that a girl would get drunk, multiple boys would have sex with her, and it would be filmed. Everyone needs to fully understand: A drunk person cannot consent, and when you are drunk, you can't protect yourself. It's fun to be a cool girl, acting like one of the guys and getting positive attention for it, matching the boys drink for drink. But the girl is going to end up way more drunk. By attempting to be an equal in this arena, the girl makes herself less equal and more vulnerable.

Encourage your kid to look out for their friends, boys and girls. Make sure it is crystal clear: A drunk person can't consent. Advocate that when they are somewhere with drinking going on, someone takes the role of staying sober and keeping an eye out for their friends. Encourage them to be aware of risks and watch out for each other. If your darling rolls their eyes at you, point out matter-of-factly, "No one sexually assaulted at a party went to that party planning on being sexually assaulted."

Important paragraph ahead...

Over and over, tell your kid that NO MATTER WHAT, you are there for them, and if shit gets real, NO MATTER WHAT they are to come to you. You are a safe place. As I've said, this only works if your kid knows they are safe from judgment and condemnation with you.

CHAPTER 11: DRUGS

Pass the Puffer Fish

We've reached the last chapter. Drugs. Probably the thing you are most afraid of. Like all Dark Lords, they are enticing. They hold the promise of a good time or a break from troubles.

This most frightening aspect of letting your kid out of the house is purposefully addressed in the last chapter. Section 2 covered emotional needs and your assignments for how to meet them in your kid. When there is a deficit in meeting those needs at home, drugs, alcohol, and other dangerous behaviors become more attractive. When you effectively parent through school issues and support them as they navigate relationships with friends and romances, the Dark Lords are less alluring. All of that work, that *PARENTING*, serves to make you less afraid of this chapter.

If your kid decides to partake in some drugs and/or that terrorist alcohol, you don't want them to do so looking for some way to feel okay. When an activity is partaken in to buffer against pain, it is more likely to become a habit or addiction.

The Drug-Free 'Merica people and War on Drugs warriors, along with the fear-peddling troubled-teen industry, proclaim that any underage drug use is deviant drug abuse and probable future addiction, and you better get them under control and into treatment if you don't want them in prison or dead. I really don't care for those peddlers of fear.

- Dolphins pass puffer fish around for a good high time. Flipper is not a deviant.
- Snails move faster when they partake in coca plants. I'm not sure who is going to tell them they still aren't getting jobs at Goldman Sachs.
- Domesticated reindeer, boldly ignoring the North Pole "Drug-Free Zone" signs, greedily partake in mushrooms and become unmanageable. Even if his name is Blitzen, he's not a bad kid.
- Cats can be total assholes. I suspect some of them would kill us if they could. However, these catnip whores will get really nice for some catnip, which serves no purpose other than to get high.

The above examples, plus several more, including stressed-out elephants hitting the hooch and war-zone water buffalo hitting the poppies, are featured in *Intoxication: The Universal Drive for Mind-Altering Substances*, by Ronald K. Siegel, PhD.

> "I just didn't know that drugs and alcohol were such a problem they had to resort to neo-McCarthyism."
>
> —DAZED AND CONFUSED (1993)

Seeking intoxication in order to not feel bad

Not only do we read about stressed-out elephants and water buffalo in Siegel's book, but also about other animals seeking relief from pain, sadness, and anxiety (just like humans do). Siegel writes, "two Hawaiian mongooses...chew the highly potent seeds of a silver morning glory...then appeared calmed for several hours. During the next few months, the mongooses ignored the seeds. Then I observed one mongoose eating the seeds again...its mate had just died and a tropical storm had reduced much of the pen to a field of mud."[14] Dammit, I love Rikki-Tikki-Tavi. I do not want him to be sad.

Much of the time discussion about teenagers and drugs focuses on rebellious behavior or being "out of control." More attention needs to be on the other "why" of intoxication: not wanting to feel like shit. People, including teenagers, drink and do drugs and smoke in order to feel better. Various intoxicants can serve to make us feel more comfortable and confident in a social setting, or relieve general anxiety, or just make things less boring. Adderall can help you get a lot done quickly, and a cigarette can feel like a friend.

Long ago and far away, I was in a volunteer training class with several other well-meaning women. When we were asked about our fears about drugs, I responded, "I am not afraid of my son smoking pot. I'm afraid of why he might be smoking pot." I perceived disapproving looks from around the table. Because I was not afraid of marijuana, they suspected I was some free-love-druggie-anarchist, which I am not.

Intoxication doesn't come only from drugs and alcohol. Siegel writes, "Dizziness is not only an ancient and adult form

---

[14] Ronald K. Siegel, *Intoxication: The Universal Drive for Mind-Altering Substances* (Park Street Press, 2005), 71.

of intoxication, it is one of the first to be discovered by children. It is common to find three- and four-year-olds whirling and twirling themselves into delirious stupors."[15] Remember those spinning metal playground contraptions? And I do love the Fantasyland Teacups. And don't forget the duct-taped-together carnival rides hitting the county fair every summer.

The opposition to marijuana legalization has sung about marijuana being a gateway drug because the hard drug addicts apparently all started with marijuana. All the people who have smoked pot and not smoked crack, meth, or heroin apparently don't count to these anti-drug warriors. If impairment is a gateway drug, maybe we should reconsider the Tilt-A-Whirl.

Even setting aside alcohol, drug use has been ubiquitous among all strata of society. Thomas Edison was a coke fiend. Robert Louis Stevenson wrote *Dr. Jekyll and Mr. Hyde* in three days, and then after his wife burned it, he rewrote it over the next three days, or some crazy shit like that. Cocaine appears to have been involved. And who believes Bill Clinton didn't inhale? That's just sort of stupid. Obama clarified that inhaling was the point. And you know George W. could party in his day.

The troubled-teen industry markets fear to parents, while at the same time alcohol marketing bombards sporting events. Greeting cards and dish towels suggest wine is how women cope with whatever is the stress du jour. While the marketing and the jokes are purportedly directed at adults, teenage humans are figuring out how to become adults. The zeitgeist clearly suggests the cool, beautiful, successful, popular adults are drinking. Why wouldn't a teenager want to be part of all

---

[15] Siegel, *Intoxication*, 211.

that? To them, tapping the keg and grabbing a red cup seems like a logical start to becoming an adult.

I know it is terrifying

I am not making light of drug use. Horribleness goes down around, and because of, drugs. Really awful stuff. Kids have overdosed on heroin and fentanyl. Kids have killed themselves and others while driving drunk. Kids have died from alcohol poisoning. Kids have died at raves. The war on drugs and DARE programs and This Is Your Brain on Drugs fried egg commercials and the Partnership for a Drug-Free America haven't destroyed the minefields. You cannot get rid of the danger. And I'm sorry; I hate it all too. I do not want your kid high, drunk, or tripping. I'm not totally on board with the rides at the county fair.

I do, however, propose that drug use (again, alcohol is a drug, people) is not deviant behavior engaged in by bad kids. It is a dangerous, potentially very dangerous, subpar choice. Your power lies in being a present and healthy parent, providing the Stability/Importance/Connection recipe, and thus minimizing the likelihood of your kid making dangerous and destructive choices.

Parent, sans war

Common parental approaches to punishing a kid for coping in an unhealthy way are sad to me. The HBO documentary *Addiction* provides some case studies of drug users. One was particularly heartbreaking. If your kid starts doing some destructive stupidness, I so badly want you to not be like this family. Teenager Dylan, who had been smoking a lot of pot, was interviewed. This kid's dad left when he was ten, and now Dylan had a really unlikable stepfather. Dylan had tried a lot of drugs and had been cutting and being aggressive toward himself. These are not the activities of a happy kid. In the interviews, neither the mother nor the stepfather demonstrated empathy or kindness toward Dylan. It was all adversarial. They didn't appear to care about Dylan; they appeared to only care about Dylan's compliance with their mandates. Their comments were soaked in righteousness. The stepfather said, "The choices that Dylan makes will either result in more freedom or a tighter box. And it's all on Dylan."

Dylan's mother had this to say: "Dylan, let's put it this way: If you give me reasons to put my thumb on you, that's your fault. And if you go crazy because you are so restricted, that's your fault, then you pay the consequences for that." I felt so bad for Dylan living with those two. Of course he wants to get high. Like the mother in Chapter 4 tousling her daughter's hair, they made *me* want to get high.

No, I am not advocating throwing up your arms and passing the crack pipe around the dinner table. I am advocating, once again, that you *double down on keeping an emotionally healthy home* and figure out what the hell is going on with your kid before doing anything else.

The troubled-teen professionals trumpet the idea that illicit drug use is abuse and you'd better get that kid into treatment. They proclaim denial is part of addiction—which may be true. Also, sometimes denial is just actual denial of something that isn't true. Don't be like the witch trial administrators using denial as evidence, as in, "of course a witch would say they weren't a witch." Listen to your kid. If they are struggling, find them a counselor who works with teenagers. Do not leap from discovering your kid is using drugs to sending them to addiction treatment without fully understanding what is going on with them. The troubled-teen industry will claim overreaction is all right. Question this. Rules and lockdowns and controls and group meetings and mandatory counseling sessions could turn into enemies and make the continued drug use an attractive alternative to misery and feeling out of control. And step back a minute before looking at programs. Do you want your kid spending more time with other kids who have been cruising the minefields?

Stare down some ugly facts

I wish we could end the chapter here, but we can't. The National Institute on Drug Abuse (part of the National Institutes of Health) conducts surveys every year about adolescent substance use rates. You can go to nida.nih.gov for a deep dive. Good news: There are long-term trends of low use of illicit substances other than nicotine, cannabis, and alcohol. Bad news: Over half of twelfth graders report alcohol (that terrorist) consumption in the last year.

Worse news: As reported by the Centers for Disease Control and Prevention in December 2022, overdose deaths are on the rise. The following comes straight from the report summary (I hate this so much):[16]

> Median monthly overdose deaths among persons aged 10–19 years (adolescents) increased 109% from July–December 2019 to July–December 2021; deaths involving illicitly man-

---

16 Lauren J. Tanz et al., "Drug Overdose Deaths Among Persons Aged 10–19 Years—United States, July 2019–December 2021," *Morbidity and Mortality Weekly Report* 71 (2022): 1581, http://doi.org/10.15585/mmwr.mm7150a2.

ufactured fentanyls (IMFs) increased 182%. Approximately 90% of deaths involved opioids and 84% involved IMFs. Counterfeit pills were present in nearly 25% of deaths. Two thirds of decedents had one or more potential bystanders present, but most provided no overdose response. Approximately 41% of decedents had evidence of mental health conditions or treatment.

All right, so far I've been all about how fear-induced overreaction won't serve your kid. Now we're going to look directly at the really ugly and the really frightening. Then I'm going to "should" some strategies at you. You are not powerless.

Priority One is to keep everyone alive

Accepting what is going on in the minefields is not condoning it, nor is it encouraging your kid to experiment with it, nor is it implying that you think your kid is going to do it. Knowledge is power. Priority One, again, is keep them alive long enough to quit doing stupid shit.

Research and understand your state's Good Samaritan laws, which legally protect from prosecution individuals who call for medical assistance for an overdose victim. Understand naloxone access and your state laws. Naloxone can temporarily reverse an opioid overdose.

> "Ketamine? It's, like, for cats—I think. It might be horses. Shit, I forget."
>
> —INCOMING (2024)

Also, both you and your kid should understand (1) where fentanyl hides in the drug supply, (2) fentanyl test strips and their limitations, and (3) signs of fentanyl or other drug overdose or alcohol poisoning.

Your kid needs to know the following, and you need to tell them this information often enough that they suspect you are playing a recording of yourself each time. I'm not opposed to neon signs.

- Fentanyl kills people—people who weren't planning to die anytime soon.
- If someone around you has any signs of fentanyl or other drug overdose, you call 911 immediately and be honest about everything you know to the 911 operator. This is being a responsible person who gives a shit about other people. A person's life is more important than worrying about protecting yourself or your friend from getting in trouble.
- Alcohol poisoning kills people. See above regarding calling 911.
- The worst part of alcohol is that it makes people do dangerous and even violent things. When you are drunk you do not have the ability to protect yourself.
- If you drink and then drive, or get in a car with someone who has been drinking, in that moment *you have decided* the following: It is okay for me to go to your funeral, it is okay for you to spend the rest of your life in a wheelchair, it is okay to go to a friend's funeral, it is okay to kill a family, and it is okay to put your friend in a wheelchair. Understand *those are the decisions* you are making when you get behind the wheel after drinking or get in the car with another driver who has been drinking.

- If you and some friends decide to drink or experiment with other drugs, and you care about one another, one person in the group stays sober, so a stupid choice is less likely to have a disastrous consequence, like a car wreck or an overdose.

Knowledge is your friend

Of course, I don't want your kids even close to these dangers, let alone trying some of them out. But Dark Lords are out there. I would very much like a world without minefields for teenagers. And people in hell want ice water. So let's deal with what IS rather than what we'd like.

Don't abdicate your influence. You lose influence when you grasp for control. I am calling on you, Dear Parent, to do more, deliberately, in your relationship with your kid and in your home to make dangerous choices less attractive to your kid. And this may enable you to get more sleep. You are *not* powerless.

Conclusion

If your kid walks in the door sobbing or you answer the phone to them crying on the other end, it's awful—for that moment you have no idea what has happened to your kid. First, be so grateful they came to you.

I've been here having coffee with you because when shit gets real I want your kid coming to you. No one loves them more than you do. I want it to be crystal clear to them that you have their back.

I have wanted for you ideas of what to do when you don't know what to do.

Whatever has gone on in your family so far is not the end. Every interaction is another opportunity to build trust and connection. Every moment is an opportunity for a new way.

There was no parent-cookie factory you were run through when you decided to raise a human. You, as a parent, are the result of your parents, and their parents, and your neighbors, and their neighbors, and so on, and so on. You are, however, now in charge of how you want to do things.

My heart goes out to you and your darlings. That is why I have been here "should-ing" left and right.

Even when it is hard, as long as you keep showing up and listening and attempting to connect with your darling no matter what, you are parenting.

If you've read something and cringed, "Ugh, I did that" or "I wish I had done that," you are in the good company of all parents who have considered how they've parented, with or without a book. If either of my kids reads this, they will for sure say, "WTF, Mom, you didn't do that." I know, and I'm sorry. Let's put it this way: My kids have known this book was in the works for a long time. Neither of them even once has said, "Yes, Mom, you should write that book."

And today is a new day. The platinum and the jewels are in the showing up in humility and loving your kid.

This parenting phase is brief. And you can totally do this.

And by Actual Experts

As I've written in the introduction, this book is coffee with a friend who has a lot to say on this topic. It is a condensed "do this, not this" book, with oversimplified "whys." It's intended to be a helpful, quick read. I've referenced several books within this book, and here are a few other books I recommend:

The Anxious Generation: How the Great Rewiring of Childhood Is Causing an Epidemic of Mental Illness, by Jonathan Haidt, is dead center on parenting issues in 2024.

Bad Therapy: Why the Kids Aren't Growing Up, by Abigail Shrier, also addresses the current issues of parenting in 2024.

For Goodness Sex: Changing the Way We Talk to Teens About Sexuality, Values, and Health, by Al Vernacchio, is introduced by the author with "I always quip that when God was passing out talents, I got ease in talking about sex."

Sex, Teens, and Everything in Between, by Shafia Zaloom, discusses the concept of consent particularly well.

In the Realm of Hungry Ghosts, by Gabor Maté, MD, explores the scientific and psychological causes of addictions and treatment alternatives.

Unbroken Brain, by Maia Szalavitz, explores addiction as a learning disorder of the brain rather than as a disease. The author has walked the path of addiction and provides an unflinching look at her experiences.

The Biology of Desire: Why Addiction Is Not a Disease, by Marc Lewis, PhD, presents problems with the disease model of addiction and how the model can obstruct recovery.

Help at Any Cost, by Maia Szalavitz, examines the dark side of the troubled-teen industry.

You may recall the book and movie *Beautiful Boy: A Father's Journey Through His Son's Addiction*, by David Sheff. The much more interesting book was the son's memoir, *Tweak: Growing Up on Methamphetamines*, by Nic Sheff. Nic Sheff provides a well-written young addict's perspective.

Acknowledgments

I am so very grateful for my two kids. First, that they exist. Next, that they appear to be willing to hang out with me. My shortcomings as a parent were numerous, and some damaging. That they now willingly spend time with me is clear evidence of Grace.

I am grateful for my kids' father. His contributions and shortcomings are neither greater nor lesser than mine. Fortunately, they are different. Two of either of us would have been unfortunate. He's kept the wheels on and his stabilizing influence (and jobs) have been critical to the whole show.

Finally, since we have to live in a world of other people's kids, I am grateful for any parent deliberately trying to parent well.

This book wouldn't have been written without Scribe Media. Everything to do with a book aside from actually writing it is daunting to me, and I wouldn't have taken it on without Scribe. Also, without the guidance and editing by Scribe editors, the book would have been incoherent. Author and podcaster James Altucher made writing a book sound easy (it's not). Listening to his podcast, *The James Altucher Show*, got me to start. Inspirational author Rob Bell provided me the confidence to write at all. His answer to anyone who says, "It's been done," is "Not by you." Thank you, all.

About the Author

Tonya Reilly's drive to seek order from chaos has led to accounting and providing Fractional CFO services, with some professional organizing on the side. She's the mother of two launched adults and has had a front-row seat watching happy teenagers and unhappy teenagers. She is also a connoisseur of self-help and emotional health media.

While being a general questioner of the status quo and the general consensus about anything, she's been a foe of the War on Drugs since she first gave it any thought. This book became an idea as an alternative to parents waging a mini "War on Drugs" in their own home and having the effort (1) be as ineffective as the big War on Drugs and (2) lead to similar unintended collateral consequences.

Tonya hikes and skis with her kids and granddaughters and is the CFO of her daughter's business. She volunteers cleaning paddocks and stalls at a horse rescue farm as she's been an undiagnosed horse girl all along. She is quite happy playing poker and making Barbie stuff.

www.ingramcontent.com/pod-product-compliance
Lightning Source LLC
Chambersburg PA
CBHW030527080526
44586CB00011B/345